SURVIVAL MINDSET

*A Guide on What to Do
When Things Go Wrong*

*Bushcraft / Survival, Emergency Planning
and Situational Awareness*

Second Edition

Peter Crittenden

SURVIVAL MINDSET

*A Guide on What to Do
When Things Go Wrong*

*Bushcraft / Survival, Emergency Planning
and Situational Awareness*

Second Edition

Peter Crittenden

SURVIVAL MINDSET

A Guide on What to Do When Things Go Wrong

Second Edition

by Peter Crittenden

Copyright © 2021 Peter Crittenden

ISBN: 9781956904079

Printed in the United States of America

Published by Blacksmith LLC
Fayetteville, North Carolina

www.BlacksmithPublishing.com

Direct inquiries and/or orders to the above web address.

This book is dedicated to all of my teachers -
most especially One-Eyed Nail,
who taught us so much down at the Barriers . . .

. . . and of course to all of those who never came back.

Contents

NOTE: The survival techniques presented within this guide focus on short-term survival, defined as less than 30 days – significantly less, perhaps 2 weeks max. This includes post-natural disaster survival (survival in place) as well as wilderness survival incidents.

For short term survival situations, a great emphasis is placed on signaling. If a comprehensive signals plan is in place in advance of whatever circumstances result in an isolating event, that situation is more likely to be less than 2 weeks.

For post-natural disaster survival, planning should be for 30 days, as the post-incident conditions are almost always worse than the initial event itself (hurricane, tornado, earthquake, tsunami, etc.) This still falls under conditions for short-term survival.

While this book focuses on short-term rather than long-term survival, primitive skills such as fabricating stone tools are presented, but I would stress readers to focus on short-term survival skills that will get you out of whatever challenging situation you find yourself in and safely back to home, sooner than later.

Foreword

Nowadays, more and more people are expressing a concern and interest in personal safety and security issues. It is my hope that this book addresses this growing interest. In presenting safety, security and survival information, a primal approach is taken – we all came from the cave, that is, humankind in nature. The natural, animal side has not left us – man is still a wild animal. One cannot separate the primitive, natural side from our daily existence; it is always there in everything we do - every observation and gut reaction - whether one is aware of it or not.

The veneer of civilization is eggshell thin. All it takes is an emergency situation of some type, a natural disaster, civil unrest, or a criminal event to bear witness to the savagery humans are capable of. Given this, I introduce a basic level of survival and security awareness skills with intent to impart a survival mindset as a strong foundation for personal security skills adaptable to any environment.

A friend and colleague once told me, "You know how it is, Pete. People like us, we're accustomed to walking into situations where there's more that we don't know than what we DO know." His words have been ringing around in my head ever since. The follow-on to what he said is that - for our kind of security professional - it's not what we know that sorts things out; it's knowing what we DON'T know (as opposed to NOT knowing what we don't know) and knowing how and where to find solutions.

I do not profess to be an expert, I am a professional outdoorsman; bushcraft and wilderness survival skills involve a lifelong journey that for me began growing up as an ex-pat kid in Sumatra, Bangladesh and Thailand in the 1960s and 70s. This foundation was built upon throughout my training and experience as a Special Forces soldier, and continues to this day as a security professional.

Foreword

The ultimate objective of this text is to impart within you - the reader - a safety, security and survival mindset. Ironically, survival mindset – the most deciding aspect of any survival situation - is a subject that cannot be taught. It can be discussed, but ultimately Survival Mindset is a human quality that must come from within oneself. It is my hope that this text can serve as the key that unlocks this capability.

Peter Crittenden
July 2021

Introduction

Consider primitive humans in the natural environment, such as the Australian Aborigines, or the isolated tribes found in remote corners of the world, such as the Amazon basin. Stone Age humans lived in small, hunter-gatherer groups of 30 to 40 individuals – roughly the size of an infantry platoon. Fewer than this made it difficult for the group to sustain itself. More than this and the group would quickly devour all food available within in any given area.

Furthermore, hunter-gatherer groups were roughly fifty percent male, fifty percent female, fifty percent adults, and fifty percent juveniles. A member of such a society spent his or her entire life looking at the same 30 or 40 persons, and would have encountered very few if any outsiders his or her entire life. Our ancestors evolved in very dangerous environment. Life was hard and filled with peril; dinner walked around on four legs, had horns and hooves that could kill you in the process of harvesting it. Close cooperation and mutual trust was absolutely necessary in order to survive. One was extremely lucky to die of natural causes at the ripe old age of around thirty-five years.

In our modern lives, as we go about our day-to-day activities in the hustle and bustle of the contemporary environment, it is quite possible to go an entire day without seeing a familiar face. In fact, it's quite a coincidence to run into someone we know in a crowded city street, or at the shopping center. It's a phenomenon we take for granted; we don't know and cannot possibly know all of the other humans that surround us. The social reality that faces modern humans is that we go about our lives surrounded by a literal sea of strangers.

Now consider; biologists have determined that it takes around 30,000 to 35,000 years for a species to display an observable evolutionary difference. The Agricultural Revolution – the single greatest event in the development of human civilization – is believed to have begun around 12,000 years ago, coinciding with the end of the last ice age. In other words, we humans are still hardwired physically and psychologically for the short, harsh and extremely violent fight-or-flight life of our Stone Age hunter-gatherer ancestors, who were surrounded by familiar faces their entire lives.

And yet, as previously described, we go about our lives surrounded by a sea of strangers. The laws, rules and regulations that define and govern civilized behavior are actually artificial constraints – but the psychological stresses modern existence imposes on us have very real consequences. Is it any wonder that we are hearing more and more of individuals who simply snap and go feral? Considering all of the above, the increasing social discord, civil disobedience, misbehavior and outright insanity we are witnessing in our modern world begins to actually make sense.

Understanding this primal source of the chaos and confusion we are witnessing within our modern society is a first step to developing personal security awareness and a survival mindset. I suggest that developing strategies for dealing with the very real hazards of modern society involves adopting the hunter-gatherer mindset of our primitive ancestors. To me, this mindset requires a comprehensive knowledge and understanding of the hard challenges of the human condition at the most primal level, and I believe the pathway to this awareness is through learning primitive bushcraft skills.

1

Principles of Safety, Survival, and Personal Security

Terrorism - Disaster Evacuations - Economic/Financial Collapse - Widespread Civil Unrest - Random/Mass Shootings - Biological Warfare - Nuclear Attack - Collapse of the Electrical Grid: these are among the greatest fears, according to the Chapman University Survey of American Fears.

More immediate threats to consider include street crime, home invasion or breaking and entering, automobile accidents and breakdowns, extreme weather, and hazards or misadventures that result in traumatic injuries. So how does one plan and prepare for all the above? One step at a time – don't try to boil the entire ocean, you'll never get there. What are the commonalities between all the above? Here are the start points for planning:

• Consider how vulnerable you are to identified threats (i.e. risk assessment).
• Develop and maintain appropriate security measures; active and passive measures to safeguard persons, equipment and property against damage, criminal and terrorist activities.
• Seek guidance regarding safety and security industry standards and criteria.

The Safety / Security Nexis

Security and safety are directly related. Consider: we wish to do things in as safe a manner as possible, and to avoid accidents. At the same time – usually without even thinking about it – we seek security on all levels, from locking the doors to our dwellings (even if we are inside them) to purchasing expensive, comprehensive insurance plans to cover every aspect of our lives. As you plan and conduct activities, seek security solutions and continually review safety risks and options.

For example, most of us have spare tires in our vehicles, but how many of us actually check the tire pressure of the spare tire? You should have a vehicle safety/self-recovery kit that includes reflective safety triangles, an air pump/battery pack with cables and clamps, a tow strap and snow/sand tracks. A first aid kit is also a good idea, plus the know-how to use it. A medical kit designed to treat serious injuries and a knowledge of trauma medicine is an even better idea.

A day hike in the woods – what could possibly go wrong? Well, let's see – you wander off trail because nature calls. You take a fall and injure your leg and cannot get back to the trail, or perhaps become disoriented and cannot find your way back.

Now you're lost outdoors on a cold night. Did you tell anyone where you're going, and what time you expect to get back? Do you have a pack with a warm coat in it? What about water and food? A means of starting a fire? A signal flare or a whistle, perhaps, for attracting attention? Do you have a compass (the magnetic compass app on your smartphone, even) and the knowledge to use it. What about a first aid kit, (and again, the knowledge to use it)?

Situation, environment and circumstances are fluid and therefore security and survival requirements change, but principles remain the same. Here are the principles that drive security operations:

• Security
• Planning
• Situational Awareness
• Control
• Common Sense

Let's explore these concepts:

A. Security

Security is your first priority; security at home, at work, during movement in between, at rest, at play, on vacation, everywhere and always. There is never enough security, and there is no such thing as 100% seamless security; you should constantly be inspecting and improving security plans and measures. A false sense of security may cause you to overlook potential vulnerabilities.

Security at home includes physical security measures such as locks on doors and hard points within your residence such as safes and strong boxes, the ability to make your home look occupied when you are not there, as well as electronic security measures such as a security system which can be monitored remotely, for example via your smartphone.

Security during movement includes practices such as maintaining situational awareness whether on foot or in a vehicle (face out of the phone or laptop, eyes on the road and your surroundings). If a passenger in a vehicle, you are actually a co-driver; know where you are going, and where you are while enroute, on a map. If driving, at traffic light stops, leaving more than a half a vehicle length between the front of your vehicle and the vehicle to your front, and being aware of possible emergency getaway pathways, to include ramming or smashing your way through to get away from there if necessary.

Travel security includes best practices such as pre-arranged pick-ups from airports, vetting your pick-up by asking him or her where they are taking you (to ensure you're not being picked up by a bad actor), awareness of common street scams, and personal security measures within your hotel against bad actors.

B. Planning

Planning – and making decisions based on your plan(s) - is a continuous, cyclical process. Planning is goal-oriented; you must identify what it is you are trying to achieve before you can develop a plan on how to get there. Planning requires identifying required resources. Planning elements include safety, security and risk management. A plan should also include control measures to assist in the execution of the plan, such as timelines, milestones, and signals. A plan should be flexible and adaptive for when unexpected events or hazards are encountered.

Planning also involve gathering information. For example, asking locals for information regarding a route you wish to take – is it safe? Will our vehicle be able to drive this road during the winter?

A communication plan incorporates the concept of redundancy; a primary means of communication, an alternate means of communication, a contingency and an emergency means of communication (P.A.C.E.). A form of communications plan that is not formally part of the P.A.C.E. is letting somebody know where you are going, and arrange a schedule of pre-planned communications, so when you fail to call in they'll know right away something's going on and they'll know where to look for you.

A final step to the planning process that is often neglected is After Action Review (AAR) and Lessons Learned. A dedicated review to identify and discuss issues (what went right, what went wrong, and what will we do different next time) is time well spent in building the foundation for planning future endeavors.

Bottom Line:

If something CAN happen, then sooner or later it WILL happen, and if it's happened before, then sooner or later it will happen again. Assume that sooner or later something will go wrong (always plan for the worst-case scenario, not the best) and then do a "what if" analysis to identify potential hazards and have a contingency planned for each one – this is basic risk management.

After-Action Review

GOAL

What are we trying to achieve?

CONTROL MEASURES

Timelines
Milestones
Communication
Plans

What do we need to do it?
What do information do we need?

REQUIRED RESOURCES

Identify Potential Threats or Hazards

RISK MANAGEMENT

Have Contingency Plans

Figure 1: The Planning Process

Write things down if necessary; lists aid the memory (the world actually does revolve around 3x5 cards). Now you have a plan, the information and tools to achieve it, and items on hand to mitigate identified threats. Use your plan – and suggestions within this guide – to develop survival and emergency kits for your home, your vehicle, your backpack, and your pocket items. The planning process is covered in detail in Section 5. Planning and Preparation.

C. Situational Awareness

On the "big picture" level this means being aware of the national economic, political - your environmental situation - and developments in your community and at your place of work. What are the trends? What are the developing hazards, shortages, and threats? What is the significance of current events? How and where is your community affected by the current political cycle? In Seoul, Korea in the late 70s to the early 90s, there used to be reports on TV and the radio about where the demonstrations were, like a sort of traffic report, so one could avoid those areas.

On a more immediate level you must develop the habit of observing and analyzing things around you and ahead of you. Be an active participant of the area you are in, not a passive bystander unaware of situations as they develop. No texting, no cell phone use while walking or driving – even as a passenger – no daydreaming. Be alert to your surroundings, be constantly sizing up your situation, and pay everything around you, from cars, to buildings, to people; "Who are those people coming towards me? Do I smell smoke?"

When we are on the phone, reading, texting or playing a game we are there not here; we tune out what's going on around us. This is okay in a safe and secure environment, such as when you are relaxing at home, but never in a survival situation which requires being 100% focus, or even a less extreme situation where certain risks exist. Don't walk with your earbuds listening to music as you walk down the street – you should be attentive to cars and people and vigilant to anything approaching you.

Keep your head up at all times and don't text while walking. Also, limit your phone conversations while you are walking so you'd be less distracted. Look at people in the street and your surroundings; you will be less likely taken by surprise.

Be aware of patterns of activity; try to 'see' what you are looking at. If a tradesman's van is parked with the driver eating his lunch for several hours, he probably is not eating his lunch; is this a surveillance operation? Unexpected visits by a plumber or a salesman could very well be attempts to gain access to your dwelling; be alert and don't be in a hurry to open the door.

Situational Awareness also means know where you are going, seek information and consult maps before you go. The advice you get may prevent an emergency situation from developing. Consult maps, seek information from multiple sources – to include the locals, look at the terrain itself. Look at the patterns of life for the area you are going through; the terrain, vegetation, wildlife, people, infrastructure, obstacles, and most importantly the weather. Is the route you plan to take suitable for your vehicle? Will the soil give for easy walking, or will it be a trudge through mud, sand or snow?

D. Control

Control measures include letting people know where you are going, what you plan on doing, and when you plan on getting back. Control also includes having a communications plan and schedule. If people know where you are going, and know to expect a call or a text at a certain hour every twenty-four hours, then they'll know where to start looking when your call doesn't come in.

What are your checkpoints along your planned route? What are your handrails, backstops, and check points?
Handrails are physical features to the left and right of an intended route, such as rivers, mountain ranges, major roads, cliffs, etc.

Backstops are physical features behind an intended destination – again; rivers, mountain ranges, major roads, cliffs, etc. – so you'll know if you've gone too far, have bypassed your destination and need to go back.
Check Points are selected features, both on your map and on the ground, to guide movement along your intended route. For example, road/stream intersections, bridges, culverts, unique terrain features that stand out, such as distinctive hills, etc.

Control measures also include never letting your gas tank go less than half full; this is so you don't have to fill up after dark in a "sketchy" part of town, and/or if you suddenly have to drive across town to a place of safety or security you've got enough gas to get there. Be aware of all the exit routes in your office, the floor of the hotel you're staying in or other places you frequent;

have in mind more than one way out in case of a fire or other danger. Check those fire stairwells; I once checked into a hotel in Hong Kong and became aware that the stairwells were being used to store furniture, they were impassable. I requested and moved to a different room on a lower floor.

E. Common Sense

The saying goes, "Common sense is not that common." That being said, there are a few commonsense guidelines that can be listed here:

• Avoid suspicious, potentially dangerous areas at night or at least have company while crossing such areas.
• Always keep your vehicle's tank at least half-full (the Half Tank Rule); this way you can avoid stopping in "sketchy" neighborhoods i.e. you've got enough gas to make it to the better, safer service station.
• Be aware of pickpockets in crowded areas, buses or subways; keep your bag as close to you as possible, fully closed and secured.
• Be very careful at ATMs; don't approach the machine if you see people loitering around the ATM – if you must use one, choose one inside a secure area, such as a bank or a hotel lobby - and never count your money in public.
• If a stranger in a car approaches you and offers to give you a ride, turn and go in an opposite direction, enter a store or retreat to a commercial building's ground floor area.
• Don't walk into an elevator with another person if you don't feel comfortable about that person, you can wait for the next elevator or take the stairs.

• Keep your car doors locked in case you have a purse, briefcase or anything of value placed on the passenger's seat; in fact, it is better to drive with your doors locked even if you don't have any valuables in the car.

A mental checklist can aid you in developing common sense guidelines for emergency planning, for outdoor excursions, or simply as you go about your daily activities. Some common sense guidelines:

I. Have What You Need

Jacks and spare tires are standard equipment in modern automobiles, but how many people have tow straps, battery packs or cables, and snow/sand track for self-recovery? There should be fire extinguishers and an evacuation plan for every level of your work and residence.

First aid kits are sold in drug stores and online, but the contents vary – most commercially available first aid kits and "survival" kits I have inspected are woefully inadequate - and a store-bought kit does not replace training, knowledge and skills. Prioritize and acquire skills, supplies and equipment based on personal and realistic expectations.

II. Use What You Have

Know how to use what you have and then use it effectively. In an emergency situation, be prepared to improvise and scavenge; junk and scrap can be fashioned into useful and necessary items. Nature provides food, shelter, fuel and other necessities when we do not have other options. Survival training greatly increases your options and capabilities.

III. Do What Is Necessary

Living in modern civilized comfort makes us soft and weak; we are reliant on technology and have subconsciously acquired habits, fears and reactions that are counter to survival necessities. Would you be willing to eat insects, earthworms or snails to survive? Fear, revulsion, fatigue, pain and false values are mental states that can result in bad decisions. This is not to say that morality, loyalty, and compassion are to be abandoned; if you survive, but in the process have abandoned your humanity you have not truly survived.

IV. RULE OF THREE's

The Rule of Three's is a tool we use to establish priorities in an emergency or survival situation.
Consider: one can survive three weeks without food, three days without water, but one can succumb to the elements (extreme heat or cold) within three hours. Ergo, shelter is first priority, followed by water, and then food.

Shelter not only means some kind of overhead cover such as a tarpaulin or a tent, but also the right kind of clothing for the environment, to include headgear. Water concerns include how to acquire water, filter and purify it, transport and store it. Food concerns include how to acquire food (traps and snares, edible plants), how to prepare and preserve it. Fire is a form of shelter and is also used to purify water and prepare food.

V. When Things Go Very Wrong

A final word on your personal safety and security; it may be that after incorporating all of the concepts discussed so far, a worst-case scenario may still manifest itself. I was once asked, "What do I do if..." and the person proceeded to describe a potential confrontation with bad actors. The answer is twofold; significantly lessen the likelihood of such a confrontation by not being in places where bad actors are, and be prepared for whatever it takes to maneuver out of such a situation, should it present itself.

The fact of the matter is there is no magic tactic or technique to defuse an aggressive attacker determined to engage in physical confrontation. Choosing to arm oneself with lethal or non-lethal weapons, or to seek physical self-defense training, are personal decisions, beyond the scope of this volume. I suggest that a rolled-up newspaper can be an improvised weapon; especially if that newspaper is wrapped around a cut-down ax handle. An umbrella also doubles as a weapon. A long stick, or a staff, can serve as a very effective weapon, especially if you know how to thrust as well as strike.

Here are two other options to move the odds into your favor:

A Taser device is an electroshock weapon used to incapacitate targets via shocks that temporarily impair the target's physical function by delivering a modulated electric current designed to disrupt voluntary control of muscles – referred to as neuromuscular incapacitation - sometimes mistaken for unconsciousness by police officers and bystanders. It functions by firing two small, barbed darts intended to puncture the skin and remain attached to the target, at a range of 15 feet. The darts are connected by thin insulated copper wire and deliver a modulated electric current.

A stun gun is a close-range form of self-defense and an effective long-range deterrent. The sound and sight of a powerful spark arcing across the stun gun's electrodes can be enough to discourage an attacker. If an assailant makes physical contact, applying the stun gun to any vulnerable part of his body and pressing the trigger will deliver a powerful charge capable of causing muscle spasms, intense pain, and possibly even temporary paralysis.

NOTE: If you choose to equip yourself with either a Taser or a stun gun, be aware that you must accept a "us versus them" mindset for self-defense. The Taser or stun gun will inflict a few moments of intense pain, during which your target will likely lose the ability to escalate the attack. This is an important advantage.

Physically, you'll need to practice producing, targeting, and deploying the weapon until you're completely comfortable with the motions. Facing a real attack, you need to respond almost instinctively - as fast as possible – training will provide this ability.

It's also important to be aware of the legal status of these types of weapons within your jurisdiction, and during travel, especially when flying. Some jurisdictions forbid the manufacture, sale, and ownership of any type of electroshock weapon; some states allow ownership of these weapons, but local city ordinances might prohibit them. Do your homework.

2

Survival Mindset and
Keyword S.U.R.V.I.V.A.L.

The first item presented within the US Army Survival Manual is Keyword S.U.R.V.I.V.A.L., which illustrates as best as possible survival mindset, or at least to provides a first step:

S - Size up your situation
U - Use all your senses, and Undo haste makes waste
R - Remember where you are
V - Vanquish fear and panic
I - Improvise
V - Value Living
A - Act like the natives
L - Live by your wits, but for now: Learn basic skills

I strongly recommend that readers who consider themselves serious students of bushcraft skills acquire their own copy of US Army Field Manual 3-05.70

(previously FM 21-76, which I helped write) and study it closely. Within this guide I present anecdotes to illustrate how attitude (i.e. survival mindset) is the critical factor in survival against almost impossible odds, while at the same time stressing the vital importance of proper planning and preparation – which of course begins right here and now – in other words; Survival Mindset.

Below are three true survival situations that reinforce key points of the Keyword S.U.R.V.I.V.A.L. and stress the significance a good survival attitude can make under challenging circumstances. These are actual events where ordinary people suddenly found themselves facing extraordinary circumstances. Hopefully we can learn from how these individuals used their wits to overcome situations that could easily have killed them, or perhaps more importantly, how prior planning or a bit of knowledge and skill may have prevented them from getting into trouble in the first place.

There are lessons present here in situational awareness, personal security awareness, planning and preparation that may apply to aspects of everyday life, situations involving travel, or even operating within urban environments.

VEHICLE BREAKDOWN, ATTEMPTED SELF-RECOVERY: Karen Klein, Bryce Canyon, Utah / Grand Canyon, Arizona, 22-24 December 2016 [1]

---

[1] How Rescuers found Karen Klein, the woman who trekked 26 miles in the snow through the Grand Canyon - by David Montero, LA Times 27 Dec 2016 https://www.latimes.com/nation/la-na-grand-canyon-rescue-20161227-story.html

S - Size up your situation
U - Use all your senses, and Undo haste makes waste

Karen Klein is a college professor in Pennsylvania (at time of this writing). She is an active tri-athlete & marathon runner. Karen Klein was on vacation in Las Vegas with husband Eric Klein, 47, and their 10-year-old son Isaac. On Thursday 22 Dec 2016 the Kleins decided to travel to Bryce Canyon in Utah and the Grand Canyon in Arizona while using GPS.

The family tried to drive on State Route 67 to the North Rim of the Grand Canyon but enroute their GPS alerted them it was closed for the winter. The GPS diverted them onto a gravel Forest Service road where their car eventually got stuck.

There was no cellphone signal. With bitter cold temperatures, the Kleins knew they had to find help fast. As Eric Klein was recovering from a back injury, the decision was made that Karen – at 46 years of age a marathon runner and triathlete – was in the best shape to make the attempt to hike out as snow kept falling. Wearing a parka, knit cap and hiking boots, she journeyed into the snow while her husband and son stayed inside the vehicle.

"I thought I'd only be gone for like an hour or two," Klein said. She ended up traversing 29 miles over the course of about 36 hours, in up to three feet of snow, before seeking shelter in a small unheated cabin where she was ultimately located.

The Kleins did not consult weather reports or seek information from hotel or tourist resources prior to setting out. Planning skills, knowledge of the limitations of GPS navigation, and a communications plan (PACE) may have prevented this event; "The GPS did not indicate that certain roads were closed and impassable," Klein said. Jim Driscoll, chief Deputy for Coconino County, Arizona, says it's a problem authorities have seen numerous times: "Google Maps shows there's a way, but it's impassable."

Karen Klein had taken wilderness survival classes, which gave her knowledge and skills that contributed to her survival; she ate aspen twigs and pine needles (pine needles contain up to 5 times the amount of vitamin C of an orange plus essential minerals that undoubtedly contributed to Karen's survival). Knowing that eating snow leads to hypothermia, Karen instead drank her own urine to avoid dehydration.

Drinking Urine: a healthy person's urine is about 95 percent water and sterile, so in the short term it's safe to drink and does replenish lost water. But the other 5 percent of urine comprises a diverse collection of waste products, including nitrogen, potassium, and calcium – therefore repeat drinking of urine can cause problems. Karen was aware not to eat snow (which leads to hypothermia) however she did place snow in her cheek to stay hydrated.

Resolution: Once the sun rose Friday, Karen resumed her hike and found an empty ranger station at a park entrance closed for the season. She broke a window with her elbow and waited inside the cabin.

Shortly after Karen had set off on her trek, Isaac Klein was able to hike to higher ground where he was able to get cellphone signal and call for help. Searchers rescued Eric and Isaac, then started an air and ground search for Karen.

Searchers of the Kane County Sheriff's Department and the National Park Service, US Forest Service & Bureau of Land Management tracker personnel found Karen Klein early Saturday morning curled up on a bed in the cabin. At that point, she was hallucinating and was too weak to stand up. Klein's rescuers gave her food and water and she was taken to the hospital, where she was treated for severe frostbite. Her husband and son were also treated for exposure and later released.

Only hours after Klein's rescue, a major winter storm hit the region that would have made it nearly impossible to find her.

Survival Mindset: Klein walked 26 miles through and over snow as deep as three feet, finding a tree to stay under Thursday night. Karen forced herself to stay awake: "I knew if I fell asleep that I would freeze to death," Klein said. "I kept thinking, this isn't how my life is supposed to end, no, no, no," she added. "My son needs his mother, my husband needs his wife. I am not letting my mother bury me . . . That instinct just kicks in, you have to protect your family. You just keep driving forward. You just have to keep moving forward."

At one point, Karen took off her left shoe to remove a piece of ice, but somehow she wasn't able to get the shoe back on. Refusing to give up, she continued without it. It took her nine hours to travel the last four miles. She'd walk 10 feet, collapse, pick herself back up and collapse again.

Rule of Three's: Sheriff's Deputy Driscoll said Karen was fortunate; in the last month, three people have died there due to exposure to the cold. "It can be a pretty hostile environment," he said, "especially at night." At about 8,500 feet, dehydration, hypothermia and exhaustion are big concerns.

Hindsight 20-20: The decision for Karen to walk out Thursday afternoon during a snowstorm was possibly flawed ("Undue Haste makes Waste"); it may have been better to stay in place for duration of the storm & walk out afterwards - preferably during early morning, to take advantage of maximum hours of daylight. Before Karen departed, they could have attempted short movements to high ground to acquire cellphone signal; this actually eventually worked, albeit after Karen departed.

SIX DAYS IN THE DESERT: Ed Rosenthal, 24-30 September 2010, Joshua Tree National Park [2]

R - Remember where you are
V - Vanquish fear and panic

Ed Rosenthal (64 years old at the time of his misadventure) was a commercial real estate broker from Culver City, California. Upon completion of a real estate deal, it was Ed's habit to go alone to the desert and hike. "I love the desert," he said. "It's just so

---

[2] Rescued Hiker Recounts 6 Harrowing Days in the Desert – by John Hoeffel, LA Times 6 Oct 2010 https://www.latimes.com/archives/la-xpm-2010-oct-06-la-me-1006-hiker-20101005-story.html

spiritual." An experienced hiker, he meant to hike for four miles at most on a trail from Black Rock Campground that he had walked at many times before. On Friday, September 24 2010, he set out to hike to Warren View.

Even though Rosenthal carried a pack stuffed with survival equipment — a whistle, matches, flares, even a space blanket, he later admitted he wasn't prepared — his large water container was only an eighth full, about a pint, he left two huge bottles in his hotel room and passed by a spigot in the park without topping off his water. After his ordeal, Rosenthal said, "When I set out, I should have not been in a rush. Like, what's the rush? To drop dead?"

On his way back through a wide-open wash, he somehow lost the trail. He scrambled through four or five canyons and strayed miles from where he started. He had a compass, but no map because he said it was a straightforward hike that he knew. In retrospect, he said a map might have helped.

In an attempt to make it out, he cut across a sunbaked hill and found a trail but missed a cutoff. He ended up in a sandy wash that funneled him into rock. Rosenthal hiked for miles as the heat became more and more intense, the landscape more and more harsh. He finally turned around and then found some shade in a small canyon and went to sleep.

When he woke, he could not remember how he got there. He clambered up rocks to get out, but he could not find the way he had come. He trudged uphill in two different directions, without luck. The heat was intense. "I stayed calm and focused. I did not get excited because if you do that then you really just drop dead," he said.

Rosenthal nestled under a tree that Saturday, breaking off branches to create shelter. Wearing just a short-sleeved shirt and shorts, the night was frigid so he covered himself with the space blanket.
On Sunday, he headed downhill to find a warmer place to camp. "I couldn't walk. My legs were finished," he said. He found a canyon with some shade and stayed put. "I made very few steps," he said. "I got weaker and weaker."

He tried to signal searchers, flashing the space blanket, blowing the whistle and using a flare to set two fires. Ed sipped the last of his water the morning after he lost his way in an isolated canyon deep in Joshua Tree National Park. It tasted sweet and delicious.

I - Improvise
V - Value Living

In the six days he survived in remote, scorched canyons, Rosenthal drank very little. "What happens is your mouth turns to like sand, and your saliva turns to sand and rocks," he said.

Rosenthal lost about 20 of his 148 pounds. He became so feeble he could not walk or sit up, not even against a rock. He ripped apart a yucca plant with a pocket knife and sucked the moisture out, but realized the task exhausted him. He tried to drink his urine, but found it disgusting.

Although not particularly devout, Rosenthal prayed. He prayed for rain, and 10 seconds later it rained. He lay down in amazement and the drops wet his parched tongue. "There was definitely a miracle. I'm much more religious now than I was. Seriously. I prayed for rain and it rained," he marveled. "My conclusion is that God is real. Really. I have to tell you. God is real."

He started to write on his floppy hat on Monday. His hat became his last will and testament; with no sign of rescuers on his third day in the Mojave Desert, Rosenthal began to write to his wife and daughter. He wrote that he made a wrong turn, ran out of water and loved them. He told them who to trust for financial advice, who should be pallbearers and who should come to his wake. He wanted a drunken, joyous party with Persian food. He wanted his ashes strewn in Topanga Canyon. He wrote a poem that started: "A brother like you is all good and true."

"I really wasn't sure I would survive," he said, but he wanted to make it for the sake of his wife of 21 years, Nicole Kaplan, and his 20-year-old daughter, Hilary. "That was my primary motive," he said.

Resolution: When he was rescued Thursday, Sept. 30, he believed he had just one more day in him.
A helicopter crew flew into the canyon about 50 feet away and hailed him. Rosenthal struggled to walk, but could not. The rescuer carried him. Back in civilization, after two nights at Hi-Desert Medical Center in Joshua Tree, everything was different. "I don't think I'm even going hiking for a long time," he said.

NOTE - Situational Awareness: A few simple measures could have prevented the misadventures described above. For the Kleins, prior planning could have involved including a Personal Locator Beacon (PLB) in the survival kit that they did not bring – this item is discussed in detail below. Blankets and other shelter, fire making materials, food and water would have also gone a long way. Most importantly they should have sought some locals' advice and let their hotel staff know their plans before they set off on a road trip that was simply undoable due to seasonal conditions. Ed Rosenthal should have topped off his water bottles before setting out (obviously) and should have also considered adding to his water-carrying capability by doubling up on water bottles, perhaps wearable collapsible water bag. A PLB would have shortened his ordeal to less than one day.

'LIFE IS WAY, WAY TOO SHORT': Plane crash survivor Autumn Veatch's story of survival in the North Cascades Mountains, Washington State – 11-13 July 2015 [3]

V - Value Living
L - Live by your wits, but for now: Learn basic skills

Autumn Veatch (sixteen-years-old at the time of her misadventure) was in a small plane with her grandparents, flying from Kalispell, Montana, to Lynden, Washington State. An hour and a half into the

---

3 'Autumn Veatch's Story of Survival', by Paige Cornwell, Seattle Times 18 July 2015 https://www.seattletimes.com/seattle-news/northwest/appreciate-the-little-things-says-teen-survivor-of-plane-crash/

flight, it started getting bumpy; then the plane dropped.

Her grandfather tried to avoid the clouds and used GPS on a tablet to see where the mountains were. The GPS malfunctioned. They went through a cloud bank, and for a few minutes, all Veatch saw was white. She crouched down behind the front seats.

"It was white, then I saw trees, then we crashed," Veatch said. For a brief moment after impact, everything was quiet. Veatch escaped before fire engulfed the plane. She isn't sure how she got out of the plane. Her grandparents were trapped in their seats. To get to her grandmother, she would have to pull her grandfather out first.

"I couldn't pull Grandpa out, because he's a lot bigger than me," Veatch said. "And I burned my hand really bad. I was starting to hurt, and it was just so hot." The smell and the panic after the couple stopped yelling for help made her want to get away. She couldn't take anything – anything and everything that might be useful for survival purposes had burned up in the wreckage.

When the sun set, she stripped down to her tank top and underwear. She tried to hang her wet clothes on branches, but they wouldn't dry. She pulled her knees to her chest, wrapped her cardigan sweater around her, tucked her head down, and breathed into her shirt to keep warm. She didn't sleep much, the burns on her hand was extremely painful. "I was certain I was going to die," she said. "I was going to die at 16 years without doing anything important with myself."

She woke up Sunday morning and walked for a few hours, then decided it was too cold. She lay down and thought "this is it." But she kept hearing a stream, which to her sounded like a highway, or a helicopter. It gave her this "weird boost of motivation."

Then she remembered something she'd learned from watching reality TV survival shows with her father: if you're ever lost in the wilderness, find a stream and follow it, because it will lead to civilization.

Survival Mindset and Survivors Guilt: "I thought, 'I can't do this to my loved ones,'?" she said. She thought about her boyfriend, her family and friends. She thought about a lot while she was in the woods. She felt selfish because she survived and her grandparents didn't. She blamed herself. "They didn't deserve to have anything happen to them," she said.

She also thought about small things: cereal, the feel of hugging someone after not seeing them for a long time, her favorite TV shows. "Appreciate the little things," Veatch said. "Those are the things you'll miss when you are in the forest, dying." She sang to herself, and talked out loud, too. She said "screw this waterfall" when she came across a 20-foot, then 10-foot cascade. She remembered the people she hadn't gotten along with, and how it all now seemed petty.

"Life is too short to hate everybody," she said. "Life is way, way too short." As she walked, she would look up and occasionally see helicopters. She waved her arms, but none spotted her. She slept on a sand bank that night.

Monday and Beyond: When she saw a bridge going over the stream she had followed, Autumn thought she was hallucinating. She scrambled up the embankment to Highway 20.

Covered in bruises and scratches and hardly able to stand, Autumn Veatch stood on the side of Highway 20 waving her arms, hoping someone would pull over and help her. For an hour, vehicles traveling across the North Cascades whizzed by her. Nobody stopped to pick her up.

Autumn Veatch had walked her way across some of the most rugged terrain in North America and had finally reached civilization, but she was still alone. "I'm hurt, I'm all burned up, but a part of me can't blame them for not stopping because I looked pretty messed up and disgruntled," she said. It was getting hard for her to stand, so she walked to the parking lot, thinking hikers might soon come back to their car. They didn't, but a red car pulled into the lot. She went up to the two men who had planned to hike.

"They were very, very, very nice about it," she said. They gave her Gatorade and snacks, and drove her to a nearby convenience store, where an employee called 911. Veatch matter-of-factly told the dispatcher there had been a plane crash in the mountains and she was the only one who made it out. She sounded stone cold in the call: "I was in shock," she said. "I had had three days to dwell that my grandparents had died." She was taken to Three Rivers Hospital in Brewster, Okanogan County, and was released the following night.

"I'm an average person that was put in an extraordinary position," she said. "Just seeing the things that I had to see, that's going to haunt me forever."

Summary

Survival Mindset is the single most important survival skill, and yet, it is the only survival skill that cannot be taught or learned from a book. It must come from within. The above survival situations teach many things: fear, anxiety, anger, frustration, guilt, despair, and loneliness are all possible reactions to the many stressors common to survival and other challenging situations. These reactions, when controlled in a healthy way, help to increase your likelihood of surviving. Do not be afraid of your "natural reactions to this unnatural situation." Prepare yourself to rule over these reactions so they serve your ultimate objective: staying alive and returning to your normal life, with honor and dignity. The challenge of survival has produced countless examples of heroism, courage, and self-sacrifice. These are the qualities that one can bring out in oneself given proper training, and mental preparation.

NEVER EVER GIVE UP

NEVER GIVE UP

3

Survival Kits

The categories for items that comprise a comprehensive survival kit also serve as a model or outline for learning bushcraft and survival skills. It's sort of like the sum is more than the whole of the parts. The categories for items that go into a complete survival kit include:

• Shelter
• Fire
• Food & Water
• Signaling
• Medical Considerations
• Movement
• Weapon or Tool
• Miscellaneous

These categories are covered in detail, each within their own section.

A. Survival Kit Types

For planning purposes, there are three types of survival kits: that which you carry within your vehicle to include vehicle recover items (and the vehicle itself, of course); that which is contained within a backpack or rucksack ("Bug Out Bag"), and items carried on your person.

For planning purposes, there are three types of survival kits: that which you carry within your vehicle to include vehicle recover items (and the vehicle itself, of course); that which is contained within a backpack or rucksack ("Bug Out Bag"), and items carried on your person.

I. Vehicle

My preferred vehicle is a diesel truck with 4-wheel drive, of course. Diesel gives you the torque for negotiating rough terrain and assisting in vehicle recovery. Diesel fuel also provides almost twice the mileage per gallon than gasoline, and diesel engines outperform gasoline engines at altitude – this becomes noticeable above 4000 feet. Preferred models would include a king cab so you can stretch out and comfortably sleep in the vehicle, if necessary.

Your vehicle should include a comprehensive recovery kit which at a minimum should include a battery power pack with cables, a jack, a tire iron or lug nut wrench, a tire plug kit, a small battery-operated air compressor for re-inflating flat tires, tow strap(s), reflective triangles, and highway flares.

3: Survival Kits

In the desert, I always include all of the above plus tools for pulling tires off rims and patch kits for inner tubes, and some lumber – 2x4 and 1x6 – to place the jack on for stability and to prevent it from sinking into soft sand or soil. I also used to pack 25 gallons of diesel fuel in 5-gallon fuel cans (jerry cans), 10 gallons of bottled drinking water, enough canned food for three or four days, thick blankets for sitting on the ground (which is HOT) and another blanket or poncho liner for sleeping under.

Where I live, we sometimes get freak snowstorms that can shut down entire sections of the highway and trap everyone in place for more than twenty four hours; my winter vehicle kit includes a small snow shovel, sleeping bag, poncho liner, food and water and a winter coat, watch cap and gloves, and a stout pair of boots if I have to walk out of there.

Snow track or sand ladders are good items for self-recovery out of sand, snow or mud, and/or the bog-out vehicle recovery straps that turn your wheels into winches, and a folding shovel, known in the military as an Entrenching Tool or simply "E-tool".

Off road considerations: if your vehicle / truck has "Traction Control" be sure to turn it off before you leave the asphalt; the chances of getting stuck in mud, snow or sand go up exponentially if you leave the traction control "On". In areas of extremely soft sand, it may be necessary to deflate your tires, at some point to where they are practically transformed into rubber tracks. For this technique, a small air compressor is required to re-inflate your tires, and possibly a bicycle air pump as a backup to the compressor.

Image 1: Off Road Anti-Skid Track

Image 2: Off Road Anti-Skid Track Snow

Images 3: Off Road Anti-Skid Track Sand

Image 4: Vehicle Self-Recovery: Wheel Winch Straps

Image 5: Spare tire used as improvised "dead man" anchor system.

II. "Bug Out Bag"   Backpack vs. Rucksack

There are many types of rucksacks and backpacks available. To keep it simple, I break it down to 2 types:

backpacks designed to carry large loads over long distances – the sort used by people who do long distance treks. These backpacks are designed to balance a heavy load via a waist strap, so the weight is transferred off the back and shoulders to the large muscles of the thighs:

Image 6: Backpack

This type of backpack towers over the shoulder. While it provides balance and comfort for carrying heavy loads over long distance, movement is restricted in dense forest or jungle terrain.

The second type of backpack or rucksack originated in the Alpine region of central Europe – probably as far back as the Roman legions – and is the basic design for military rucksacks:

Image 7: Rucksack

This type of rucksack sits does not rise above the shoulders. While not able to balance quite as well as the larger backpack, a frame keeps the rucksack off the back and a waist strap helps transfer the weight off the back and shoulders to the thighs. The rucksack carries less volume but is more maneuverable in dense foliage and allows movement of the head and neck in all directions even when laying in the prone – an advantage for military purposes.

For "Bug Out Bag" purposes I recommend the latter (rucksack) over the former (backpack) because it's smaller (for stashing in a vehicle) and is easier to don, move and carry about. Because of its basic "teardrop" shape, it is less prone to getting snagged or caught on vegetation. Bear in mind, your "bug out bag" is a survival kit, not a house on your back, and despite the generally smaller size, it's possible to jam in a sleeping bag and even a small shelter, and still have room for your other survival items.

Military Rucksacks

My personal preference is the venerable US Army A.L.I.C.E. (All-purpose Lightweight Individual Carrying Equipment), which is a direct descendant of the alpine-style rucksack:

Image 8: A.L.I.C.E. (Large) Rucksack

It seems that as long as I was in the Army, the Army was trying to redesign and replace the ALICE, but we kept going back to it. They finally introduced a replacement rucksack – the MOLLE (Modular Lightweight Load-carrying Equipment) 4000 - and I'm not a fan, but at the end of the day a lot of it comes down to personal preference.

Image 9: M.O.L.L.E. 4000 Rucksack

Nominal volume of the MOLLE pack without auxiliary pouches is 4000 cubic inches (hence its name), while the ALICE is approximately 3800 cubic inches including the exterior pockets. The MOLLE appears to be made of 500d Cordura throughout, while the ALICE pack is 200D Nylon; thinner and much lighter (especially when wet). The ALICE is a simpler system with not as many straps and buckles as the MOLLE.

I like the ALICE because it's about half the weight of the MOLLE, it doesn't rise over the shoulders, and the tubular aluminum frame seems to create more airspace between the rucksack and my back than the MOLLE. Both rucksacks have outer loops for fastening items externally, either with parachute cord, zip ties or other fasteners. (**NOTE**: if you fasten items with zip ties, back it up with para cord because zip ties will eventually fail). In the photo above, the ALICE pack has been modified – the old metallic "fiction adaptors" have been replaced by modern "fastex" plastic fasteners – we used to pay our parachute riggers with beer to modify our rucksacks like this.

Packing

"Ounces make Pounds" is the basic principle behind loading your rucksack. Try to keep it simple – I avoid as many "cool gadgets" as possible, instead focus on items that are multi-purpose – and consider that beyond what is required for 72 hours, it is almost impossible to carry more.

Heavy items go to the top, for balance purposes. Items you will need first must be accessible in the top, top flap, outer pockets or strapped onto the outside. First aid / trauma medical kits fall into this category. Shelter items such as a tarp may be strapped tight under the top flap where they are readily accessible and as an added plus keep rain off the main bag.

Pack items inside within one or more heavy duty waterproof bags – this keeps your stuff dry, and aids in floatation if fabricating a poncho raft from your rucksack. If you are packing extra footgear (such as a pair of running shoes for some relief after marching in heavy boots all day) put them in the bottom to provide structural support to the load, and because you'll need them last. Of course, bear in mind that for a "bug out bag" designed around short-term survival, an extra pair of shoes is a luxury, not a necessity.

I always carry at least one extra rucksack strap (an advantage of the ALICE rucksack is that the straps can be purchased separately) and some extra para cord for repairs, for when a strap blows out on you.

III. Items Carried on Person

The third type of survival kit is items carried on your person, or in your pockets.

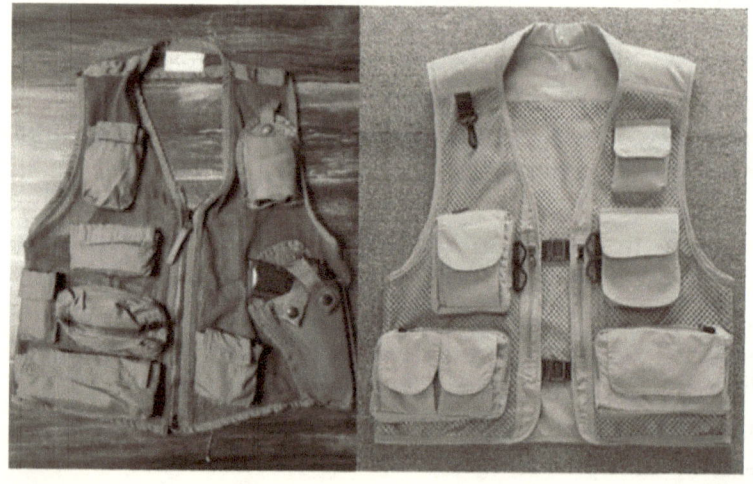

Image 10: Survival Vests – Military Aviators (L); Civilian (R)

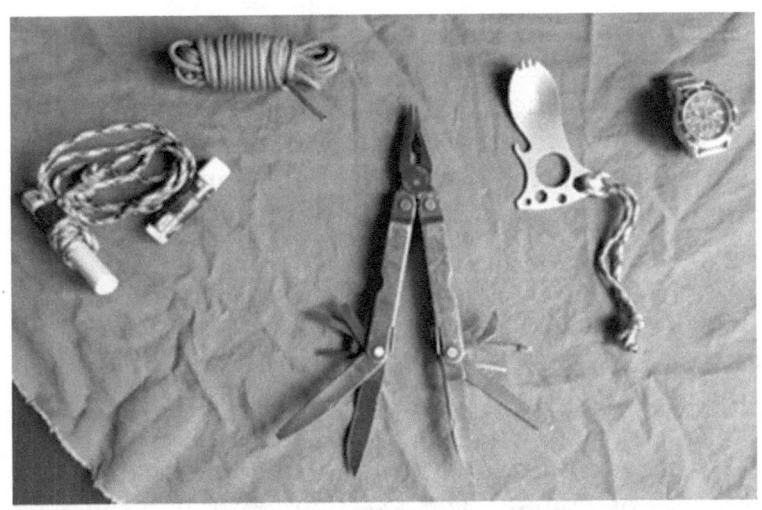

The advantage of a vest system is that more items can be carried than normally within the pockets of one's shirt and trousers. Of the six random pocket items displayed above, all of the Survival Kit categories are represented:

Shelter - the 550/paracord plus the green "Drive-On Rag" represent shelter, the multi-tool also represents the means to create a shelter, and the lip balm also represents a form of shelter.
Water - the "Drive-On Rag" can be used to collect and/or filter water.

Food - the 550/paracord plus the multi-tool represent the means to create traps and snares, and the multi-tool can also be used to kill & clean small game.
Fire - the disposable lighter plus the multi-tool represents the means to build a fire.

Signaling - the disposable lighter plus the multi-tool represents the means to build a signal fire.

Primitive Medicine - the "Drive-On Rag" and the multi-tool represent means to perform primitive medical procedures, and the disposable lighter may be used to build a fire for sterilizing the multi-tool and boiling water.

Navigation - the wristwatch may be used to find direction, any time of day in the Northern or Southern hemispheres.

Weapon or Tool - the multi-tool represents this category, of course. The 550/paracord may also be used to fashion primitive weapons or tools, and the "spork" is also a tool; not only as an eating utensil but it also includes hex wrenches and a screwdriver in its handle.

Miscellaneous - everything here is "miscellaneous".

B. Survival Kit Categories

In putting together, a survival kit, remember the categories:

• Shelter
• Fire
• Food & Water
• Signaling
• Medicine / First Aid
• Movement
• Weapon or Tool
• Miscellaneous

Image 11. Survival Kit Items

There should be redundancy for all items within your survival kit, as much as possible. All items should have at least two purposes. For example, an orange & silver "space blanket" can double as a ground-to-air signal panel. A canteen cup can serve as a container to hold various items, a water collection device, and as a pot to boil water for purification and cooking. A knife is only a knife, but a multi-tool is a knife, and a saw, and a file, and several types and sizes of screwdriver, and an awl, and a can opener, and a wire stripper, and a wire cutter, and a set of pliers. A multi-tool doesn't replace a tool kit, but it sure helps when you don't have a tool kit.

I. Shelter

The Rule of Threes is: a person can survive up to three weeks without food, three days without water, but exposure to the elements can take a person down within three hours. Therefore, shelter is the highest priority within the categories of a survival kit.

II. Fire

A survival kit should include waterproof matches ("lifeboat" matches), a magnesium or ferrocerium rod and striker, and accelerants such as camping fuel cubes, candles or petroleum jelly and cotton wool.
Firecraft is an art in and of itself, and the skill of creating fire without any of the above, via fire plows and fire drills, is a skill worth mastering that requires a LOT of patience.

III. Food & Water

We revisit the Rule of Threes: a person can survive up to three weeks without food, three days without water, but exposure to the elements can take a person down within three hours. Shelter is primary of course, but water is close second for short-term survival.
With Water, we are concerned with how to acquire, purify, store and transport it. The same applies to Food, with the additional abilities to be able to prepare it and preserve it.

IV. Signaling

Signaling includes two sub-categories: electronic and visual (non-electronic). Electronic capabilities are discussed in depth, later in the text.
Visual signal items contained in a survival kit include signal mirrors, Ground-to-Air signal panels, signal flares and the means to create signal fires.

V. Medicine / First Aid

Medical items include medical supplies, medications such as pain killers, antibiotics, antipyretics, anti-diarrhea medication and antimalarials but also multiple-use items that may have use as primitive medicine, such as salt. Any kind of instructional material is also useful, as well as medical training, of course.

VI. Movement

Movement items include compass, maps, GPS, and phone app with maps and geolocation (recommend GIS surfer Interactive Maps and Maps.me app), a knowledge of celestial navigation (which is direction finding using the sun and the stars) and other expedient direction-finding methods, and last but not least a stout pair of walking shoes or boots.

VII. Weapon or Tool

This category refers to items that allow one to fabricate weapons or tools. The ability to create improvised tools and equipment is a vital skill in any survival situation. Examples include rope, rucksacks, clothes, nets, and so on. By weapon, the meaning is a weapon suitable for hunting and capable of dispatching small game.

VIII. Miscellaneous

One is limited by their imagination, of course. A few miscellaneous items to include in any and all survival kits or "bug out bags" (not presented in any order of importance or priority):

- Parachute cord (550 cord – at least 60 feet)
- Poncho Liner ("woobie")
- Duct tape
- Electrical tape
- Small disposable lighters
- Pencil and pad of paper
- A sharp knife, and a means to sharpen it (nothing is more useless than a dull knife)
- Multi-tool
- Small flashlight + spare batteries
- Small collapsible shovel, or "E-tool"
- "Zip-lock" plastic bags
- Sweat rag or cravat
- Medical shears
- Metal canteen and/or canteen cup (suitable for boiling water)

4

Planning and Preparation

To reduce risk, we develop plans. In the planning process, we consider consequences of action and/or inaction. Establishing acceptable and unacceptable risk levels to manage anticipated impacts increases risk capacity and resiliency. Emergency preparedness mitigates risks by recognizing and understanding key threats, and by acquiring practical tools, training, resources, timely information and reference materials.

A. The Planning Process

Steps in the planning process include:

• Establish goals (setting objectives); what is it you are trying to achieve, or where do you plan on going and what do you want to do when you get there?

• Determine tasks required to meet the plan's objectives; what do you need to do (or know) to accomplish your plan?

• Identify required resources; what will you require (time, tools, information) to achieve your objective(s)? How are you going to get to where you are going? What is your security plan? What is your supply/resupply plan? What is your medical plan?

• Develop planning premises (assumptions, knowns and unknowns): What do you know about what you are trying to achieve, obstacles to overcome, or about where you want to go? What are the foreseen critical events and decision points? Specifically, what do you NOT know, and how can you get that information (did you seek local information regarding routes, weather conditions, hazards, etc.)?

• Risk management; what are the possible risks or hazards that exist or that you may encounter along the way – WRITE THEM DOWN - and what measures have you taken to mitigate those risks? Alternate courses of action; what's your plan for when and if you encounter hazards?

• Control measures; what's your communications plan - Primary, Alternate, Contingency, Emergency (PACE)? What is your route plan (checkpoints, left and right handrails i.e. rivers, streams, road/stream intersections, ridgelines, physical objective on the ground) and is there an alternate route? Other measures in managing the safe and secure conduct of your plan include letting someone know where you plan to go and when you expect to be back, so they know where to go looking for you when you fail to check in.

Incorporate the 5 W's (+ How Many) to develop a sample format for planning an outdoors event or excursion:

WHO: Names of party members, phone numbers, family or significant other contact information, medical and other considerations.

WHAT: Activity, or destination.

WHERE: Location, route plan, and alternate routes.

WHEN: Departure or start time, timelines enroute, planned communications, and no-later-than time expected to return.

WHY: Purpose of event (e.g. training, recreation, information-gathering).

HOW MUCH or HOW MANY: How much food and water, fuel and other resources are required.

Here are some examples of planning considerations:

Required Tasks: Hike twelve miles with a 50lb (22.7kg) backpack. Drive a vehicle. Read a map and navigate to a known point. Pitch a tent. Build a fire. Find and purify water. Send and receive electronic communications.

Time, Tools, and Information Required: How long it will take to get to your destination (or to accomplish your task), how long you expect to be gone, and when you expect to be back. Necessary tools and equipment may include outdoors gear, boots, clothing, vehicle and recovery equipment. Have you consulted a map and asked locals for information - this principle goes hand-in-hand with Situational Awareness, as oftentimes you plan your route while inspecting maps and seeking information from other sources – and do you have a compass, GPS (and the ability to use them)?

Assumptions (Knowns and Unknowns):
Distance can be measured on a map but what is the condition of the road/path/trail or off-road conditions? How long will it take to travel under good conditions? How long will it take to travel under adverse weather? Is the route passable in winter? Are food/water/fuel resupply points confirmed?

Risk Management: Possible risks or hazards include: A) injuries due to falling on steep, uneven terrain, B) heat-related injuries, C) snakebite, D) becoming lost and/or isolated. Measures to manage or mitigate these hazards include: A) medical supplies and training, plus signal devices, B) water and rest plan, C) if encountered, do NOT handle snakes, avoid thick undergrowth, wear boots and long trousers, have medical supplies and knowledge to use them, and ability to call for medical evacuation. D) Maps and compasses, navigational skills, plus signal capability to search & rescue organizations. Alternate courses of action may include shortening the route or taking an alternate route (previously identified) if the primary route is impassable or party must return sooner than originally planned.

Food & Water: How much food is required? Can it all be carried, or is food resupply available along the way? Where are the water resupply points? Is the water potable, or do you have the ability to filter and purify it?

Fuel Plan: When driving long distances off-road – across a desert, for example – how much fuel is required to get to your destination, and what is your Point of No Return (PONR) if you stray off-track (i.e. the point beyond which you can no longer go back to refuel, therefore there must be a fuel point within range of how much fuel you have left)?

Medical: Every member of the party carries a first aid kit and is trained to use it. A trained Wilderness First Responder (WFR) is present, equipped with a trauma kit that includes splints, tourniquets, pressure bandages, airway, etc.

Control Measures: Route plan includes checkpoints (start point, rest areas, road or trail intersections and bridges), left and right handrails (rivers, streams, ridgelines), and destination identified on map. Families and local park rangers will be informed someone of where we plan to go and expect to be back. Communications plan (P.A.C.E.) = cellphone (Primary); Two-Way Satellite Messenger (Alternate); Personal Locator Beacon (Contingency); Signal flares, signal mirrors, signal panels, signal fires (Emergency).

B. Prepare Now, for Emergencies Later

Are you confident that you're prepared to prevent and/or respond to emergencies, natural disasters and criminal/terrorist activities? What training, tools, and "best practices" familiarization are necessary to develop one's personnel security awareness and emergency preparedness?

Seek training, guidance, and advice for things that you don't know or are not confident in your skillset. Use this guide to determine what you need to know.

As earlier discussed, the single most important variable in an emergency or crisis is one's mindset and behavior. While this mindset cannot be taught in a classroom or learned from a book, it is possible to develop situational awareness through training, and to learn planning skills and techniques in order to be prepared for when emergencies – natural or man-made - occur.

The following skills and items should be worked on and acquired now, to be prepared for any future emergency or survival situations:

• Survival Mindset
• Security and Situational Awareness
• Survival Kits – types and categories
• Shelter - to include suitable clothing, and how to construct shelters if necessary
• Water – how to acquire it, filter and purify it, transport and store it
• Food – how to acquire it, prepare and preserve it, and store it
• First Aid and Trauma Medicine
• Signaling and Communications – to include developing and maintaining a

Primary/Alternate/Contingency/Emergency (PACE) communications plan
• Land Navigation —how to use a map and compass and/or GPS, how to measure distance via pace count, and expedient navigation skills.

Situational Awareness is noticing locations, conditions, and actions in one's environment; skills we use every day. Personal Security Awareness involves the knowledge of threats, criminal strategies and scams, in order to foresee situations as they unfold and to avoid undesirable outcomes. Seek training in how to be vigilant to help expand and improve perception of what is happening around you in situations of heightened risk in order to more effectively avoid negative consequences, and to exploit opportunities.

Ultimately, the key to emergency preparedness is not what items you have or what skills that you know, it's knowing what you do not have and do not know and knowing where to access those items and that information now, before they are needed. For example, prior to inclement weather, you should prepare your home by having ample food and water supplies, a propane camp stove to prepare food and a wood burning stove for heat when and if the power goes out. Before embarking on a hike or a road trip to a remote site, consult maps and seek information from locals. Let someone know where you plan to go, and establish a communications plan so people will know where to look for you when you fail to call in.

5

Shelter

According to the Rule of Threes, a person can survive up to three weeks without food, three days without water, but exposure to the elements can take a person down within three hours. Therefore, shelter is your first priority in a survival situation.

Fire is a form of shelter (for warming your body and drying your clothes) as well as a method for purifying water, preparing food and signaling for help. As a primary survival skill, firecraft is addressed within its own section of this guide. Learn how to build a fire even in wet or snowy conditions. Even if you have no fire or food, an adequate shelter that is warm and dry will keep you alive until rescuers find you; anything from an overhanging rock shelf to a cave, a timber lean-to or snow cave. Always prepare for the worst and build a shelter that will last. Cut boughs from evergreen trees and use them as padding and for covering.

The human body is comparatively fragile without protection from the elements. Our bodies function best when core temperatures range from 35.6 to 38.9°C (96 to 102°F). Three key factors that affect body temperature are ambient temperature, wind (wind chill), and moisture (dew point). Understanding how heat is transferred and methods to control it can help you to maintain your body's core temperature.

Be aware that we require shelter from extreme heat as well as from the cold. This means not only shade from direct sunlight but insulation from the kind of hot, dry heat found in desert and arid environs. While shorts and a thin T-shirt are ideal for humid, tropical environments, in a desert the challenge is to put shade over as much of your skin as possible, to prevent water loss through perspiration. This is why desert people dress in long, loose flowing robes.

A. Types of Body Heat Transfer:

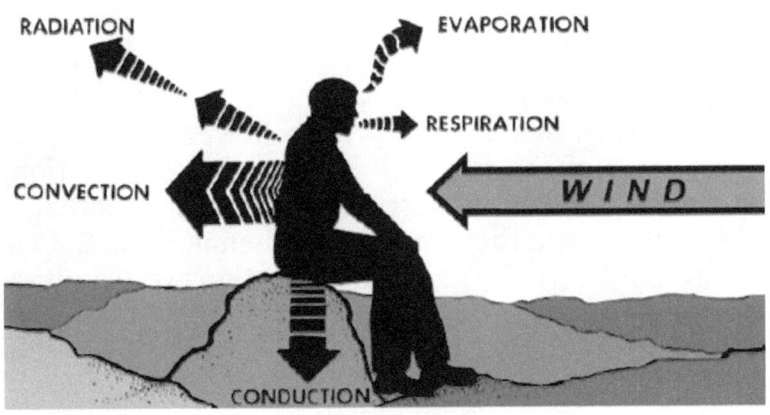

Figure 5-1: Body Heat Transfer

• Radiation — this is the primary cause of heat loss, defined as the transfer of heat waves from the body to the environment and (or) from the environment back to the body.

• Conduction – this can be defined as the movement of heat from one molecule to another within a solid object.

• Convection — heat movement by means of air or wind to or from an object or body is known as convection.

• Evaporation — this is the process by which liquid changes into vapor, and during this process, heat within the liquid escapes to the environment.

• Respiration — the respiration of air in the lungs is also a way of transferring heat. It works on the combined processes of convection, evaporation, and radiation. When breathing, the air inhaled is rarely the same temperature as the lungs. Consequently, heat is either inhaled or expelled with each breath.

In a survival situation, your chances of suffering an injury related exposure to heat or cold are great, due to injury, stress, and lack of proper clothing or shelter. These type of injuries – hypothermia, dehydration, heat cramps, heat exhaustion, heat stroke, chilblains ad frostbite - and their treatment when medical help is not available are covered under Section 10. Primitive Medicine.

B. Methods of Personal Protection

Clothing is your first means of shelter in a survival situation will be the clothing you wear. This point is true regardless of whether you are in a hot, cold, tropical, desert, or arctic situation. The US military uses the **C-O-L-D-E-R** acronym:

C – Keep clothing **CLEAN**:

In winter, it is also important from the standpoint of warmth. Clothes matted with dirt and grease lose much of their insulation value. Heat can escape more easily from the body through the clothing's crushed or filled up air pockets.

O – Avoid **OVERHEATING**:

When you get too hot, you sweat, and your clothing absorbs the moisture. This affects your warmth in two ways: dampness decreases the insulation quality of clothing, and as sweat evaporates, your body cools. Adjust your clothing so that you do not sweat.

L – Wear your clothing **LOOSE** and in **LAYERS**:

Wearing tight clothing and footgear restricts blood circulation and invites cold injury. It also decreases the volume of air trapped between the layers, reducing its insulating value.

D – Keep your clothing **DRY**:

In cold temperatures, your inner layers of clothing can become wet from sweat and your outer layer, if not water repellent, can become wet from snow and frost melted by body heat. Wear water repellent outer clothing, if available.

E – EXAMINE your clothing for worn areas, tears, and cleanliness.

R – REPAIR your clothing early before tears and holes become too large to patch. Improvised sewing kits can be made from bones, plant fibers, para-cord (550 cord), and large thorns.

In cold weather environments, dress in layers and take extras with you. Put on layers before you become chilled and take off a layer before you become damp with perspiration. Staying warm is a process of staying dry. Do not dress in cotton - it becomes wet easily and is difficult to dry. Use wool, wool blends or synthetic clothing that wicks moisture away from skin.

Winter headgear should conserve heat, breathe and be water repellent. Have a cap that made of wool or synthetic fleece; up to 45 percent of your body's heat is lost around your head, neck and shoulders. Use waterproof footgear, wool or synthetic socks, and always remember to carry gloves.

Lightweight space blankets provide temporary shelter from the cold. A larger survival kit can contain a poncho liner ("woobie") or even a sleeping bag, warm woolen watch cap, scarf and gloves, or for hot weather, a tarpaulin (for shade and shelter from rain) and a sun hat ("boonie hat").

C. Improvised Shelters

The type of shelter required will vary with location and situation. Four prerequisites must be satisfied when selecting a shelter location:

• A shelter needs to be near water, food, fuel, and a suitable site for signaling and potential recovery.

• It must be safe, providing natural protection from environmental hazards (i.e. timber dead falls, rock slides, mudslides, avalanche, flash flood etc.).

• Sufficient materials must be available to construct the shelter.

• In some cases, a natural shelter may already be present; this will save time and energy. Do not limit yourself by assuming that shelters must be a fabricated. This does not rule out shelters with a fabricated framework, it simply enlarges the scope of what can be used as a survival shelter.

• The area chosen must be both large enough and level enough to accommodate however many persons are in the survival party.

In constructing a shelter, consider the length of expected stay - short-term versus long-term – do not put more time and effort into building a structure than necessary; there are other survival tasks such as building a fire, gathering food and water, or signaling. Improvised shelters can be erected quickly with minimal effort using both man-made and natural materials; layers of branches with leaves piled between, tarpaulins, plastic garbage bags, space blankets, etcetera. Lightweight space blankets can used to reinforce a waterproof layer in a leaf shelter.

Natural formations such as caves, rocky crevices, clumps of bushes, small depressions, large rocks on leeward sides of hills, large trees with low-hanging limbs, and fallen trees with thick branches can provide shelter a basis for creating an improvised shelter.

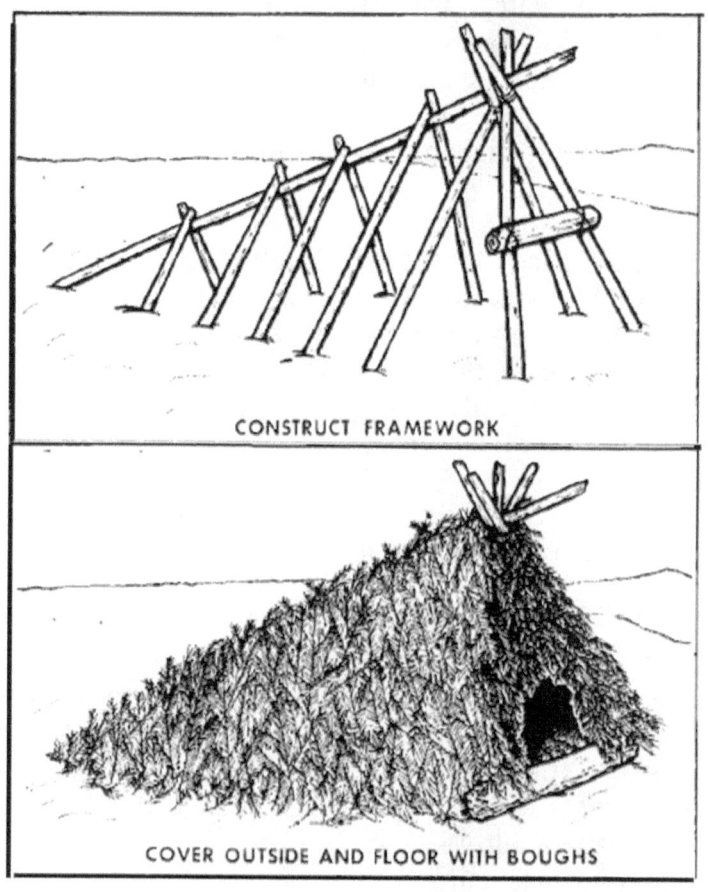

Figure 5-2: Basic A-Frame Shelter Construction

Figure 5-3: Basic A-Frame Shelter Construction

When selecting a natural formation avoid low ground such as ravines, narrow valleys, or creek beds, because of the threat of flash flooding. Low areas also collect the heavy cold air at night and are therefore colder than the surrounding high ground. Thick, brushy, low ground harbors snakes and insects; check the area for poisonous snakes, ticks, mites, scorpions, stinging ants, etc. Look for loose rocks or dead limbs that may fall on your shelter.

In tree-covered areas, sufficient natural shelter building materials are normally available. Caution is required. Shelters built near rivers and streams may get caught in the overflow. Tree-line area shelter types include A-Frame and lean-to or wedge construction.

Figure 5-4: Lean-to Shelters

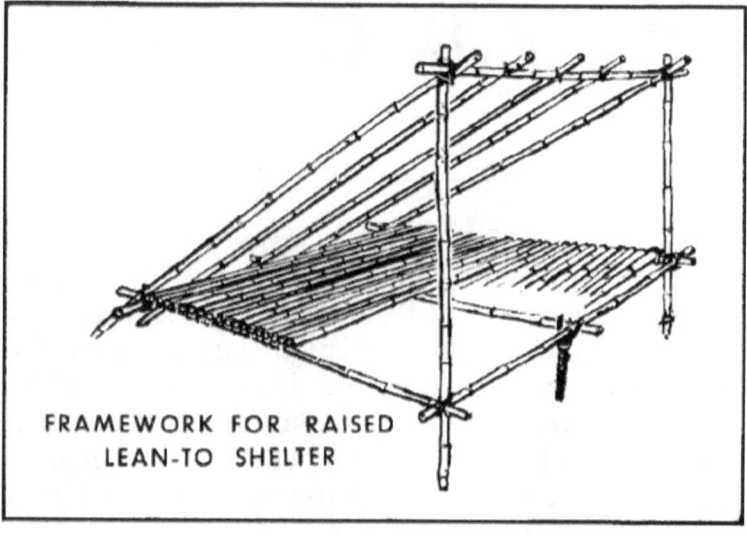

FRAMEWORK FOR RAISED
LEAN-TO SHELTER

For tropical environments, constructing a raised sleep platform and/or using grass, leaves or pine branches for insulation from the ground may improve comfort and provide some protection from harmful insects and snakes. A fire wall increases the heat gained from a fire by reflecting it back towards the shelter.

Snow cave is a shelter suitable for barren-type areas.

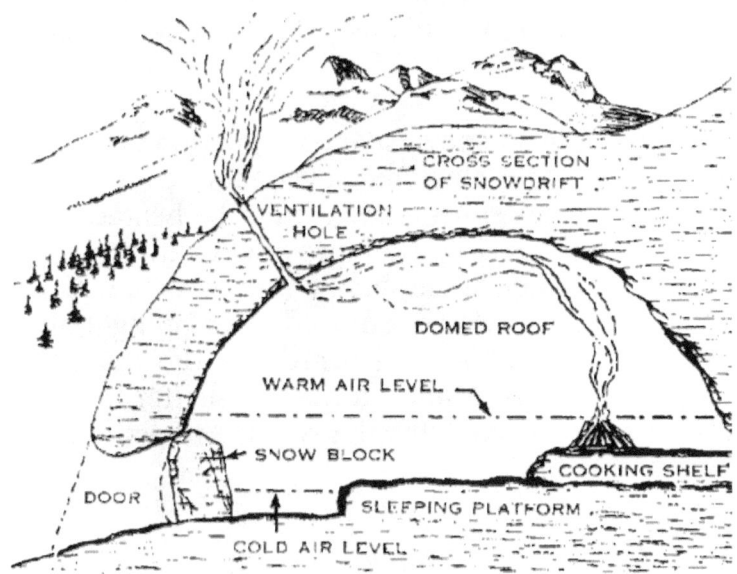

Figure 5-5: Snow Cave

All openings except ventilation holes should be sealed to avoid heat loss. Leaving vent holes open is especially important if heat producing devices are used. Candles, Sterno, or small oil lamps produce carbon monoxide. In addition to the ventilation hole through the roof, another may be required at the door to ensure adequate circulation of the air. (As a general rule, unless persons can see their breath, the snow shelter is too warm and should be cooled down to preclude melting and dripping.)

Regardless of how cold it may get outside, the temperature inside a small well-constructed snow cave will probably not be lower than -10°F (-23.3°C). Body heat alone can raise the temperature of a snow cave

45°F (7.2°C) above the outside air. A burning candle will raise the temperature 4 degrees. Burning Sterno (small size, 2% oz) will raise the cave temperature about 28°F (-2.2°C).

A critical step in snow cave construction is to dig a sump below the sleeping level, for cold air to accumulate. Since snow caves cannot be heated many degrees above freezing, they provide a rather rugged life. Once the inside of the shelter "glazes" over with ice, this layer of ice should be removed by chipping it off or a new shelter built since ice reduces the insulating quality of a shelter. Maintain the old shelter until the new one is constructed. It will provide protection from the wind.

I. Knots

To be able to construct shelters, traps and snares, weapons and tools, and other devices; a basic knowledge of ropes and knot tying is required. A good knot must pass three tests: 1) It is easy to tie, 2) it stays tied, and 3) it is easy to untie.

Some of the terms used with ropes and knots include the following:

• **Bight**: A simple bend of rope in which the rope does not cross itself.

• **Lay**: The lay of the rope is the same as the twist of the rope.

• **Loop**: A loop is formed by crossing the running end over or under the standing end to form a ring or circle in the rope.

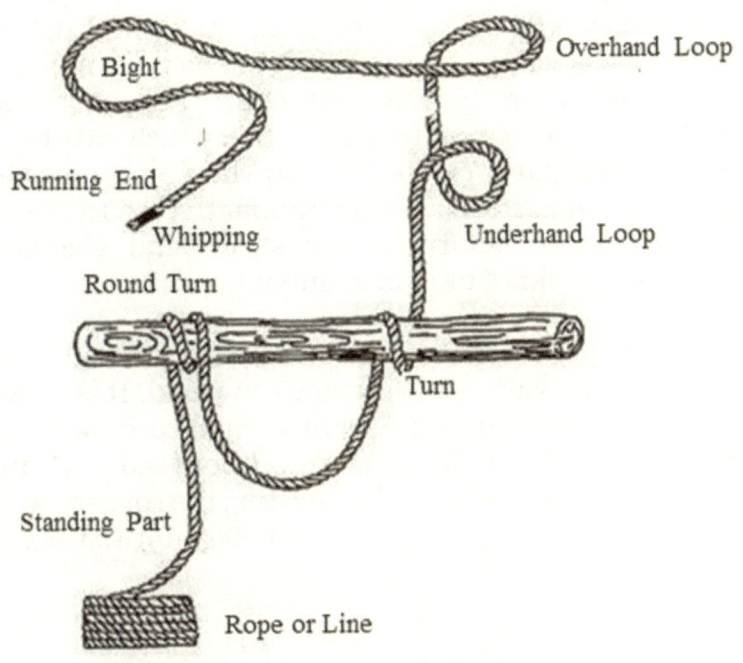

Figure 5-6: Terms used with Ropes and Knots

• **Running End**: The free or working end of a rope. This is the part of the rope you are actually using to tie the knot.

• **Standing Part**: The static part of rope or rest of the rope besides the running end.

• **Turn**: A loop around an object such as a post, rail, or ring with the running end continuing in the opposite direction to the standing end. A round turn continues to circle and exits in the same general direction as the standing end.

• **Dressing the Knot**: The orientation of all knot parts so that they are properly aligned, straightened, or bundled. Neglecting this can result in an additional 50 percent reduction in knot strength. This term is sometimes used for setting the knot which involves tightening all parts of the knot so they bind on one another and make the knot operational. A loosely tied knot can easily deform under strain and change, becoming a slipknot or worse, untying.

• **Whipping**: Any method of preventing the end of a rope from untwisting or becoming unwound. It is done by wrapping the end tightly with a small cord, tape or other means. It should be done on both sides of an anticipated cut in a rope, before cutting the rope in two. This prevents the rope from immediately untwisting.

Figure 5-7: Whipping

Whipping intends to stop a rope end from unraveling. Tie a rope end with a simple over hand knot and wrap it with duct tape for a temporary fix. A whipping knot uses twine to bind natural-fiber rope.

Figure 5-8: Heat Fusing Nylon Rope or Paracord.

Heat fusing with flame melts the end of artificial-fiber rope or cord made of plastic or nylon (such as para-cord). I have listed below 12 knots, useful for constructing shelters, traps and snares, weapons and tools, and other purposes, and how to tie them.

Mastering each of these knots to memory, to where on could tie them in the dark even, would take a significant period of time. While you work on the 12 knots, I suggest that it's possible to get by with 3 basic knots; a) Square Knot, b) Round-Turn and Two-Half-Hitches, and c) Trucker's Hitch. These three are included below.

• **Square Knot**: The square knot is good, simple knot for general purpose use, used to tie the ends of two ropes of equal diameter together.

Figure 5-9: Square Knot.

The square knot is basically two overhand knots that are reversed:

Figure 10: Overhand Knot.

"Right over Left, Left over Right", and then secured with an overhand on both ends. It is easy to inspect, as it forms two loops and is easy to untie after being loaded. Two more overhand knots secure the free ends, as a square knot will untie itself when not under tension.

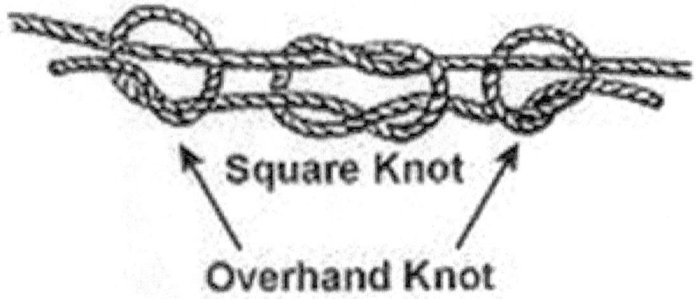

Figure 5-11: Securing the ends of a Square Knot.

• **Round Turn and Two Half Hitches**:

Figure 5-12: Round Turn and Two Half Hitches.

Round Turn and Two Half Hitches is a main anchor knot for one-rope bridges and other applications, most used to anchor rope to a pole or tree.

• **Trucker's H itch:**

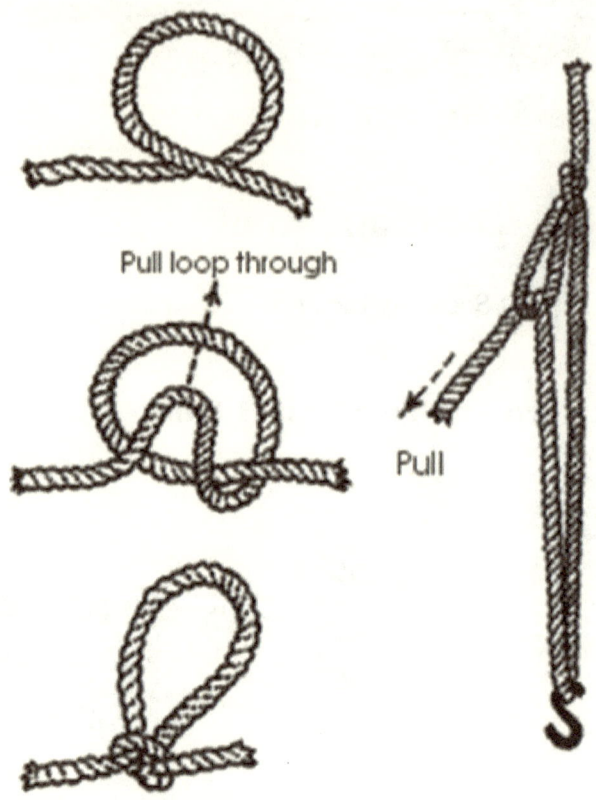

Pull loop through

Pull

Figure 5-13: Trucker's Hitch.

Use the trucker's hitch to cinch down a load, or to tighten and secure the ends of a shelter. This combination of knots allows a line to be pulled very tight. Tie one end of rope to fixed object such as car bumper or a stake in the ground.

About mid-way on the rope tie a slippery half hitch to form a loop in the middle of the line. Be sure the loop part is formed with the slack part of the rope or it will tighten down on itself under pressure. Make a wrap around another fixed point opposite the tie-in point and feed free end through the loop. Using the loop as a pulley, pull down with the free end as tight as you can and secure the knot with two half hitches around one or both lines.

• Clove Hitch, End-of-Line Clove Hitch:

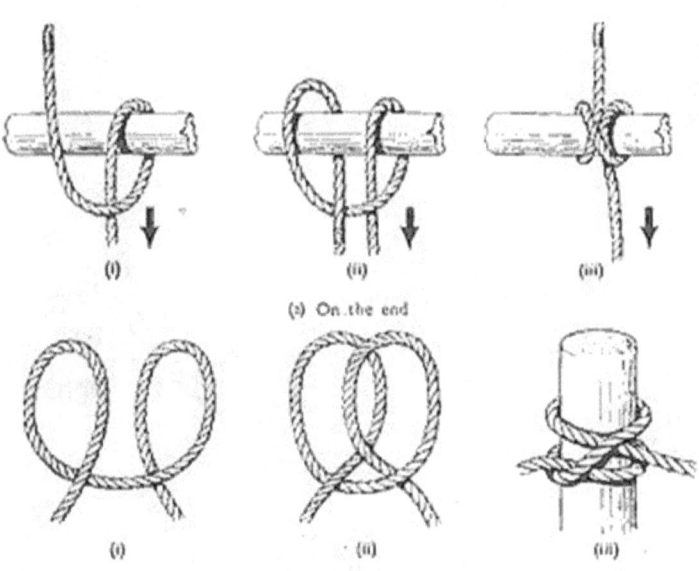

Figure 5-14: Clove Hitch; End-of-Line Clove Hitch.

Clove hitch and end-of-the-line clove hitch can be used to fasten a rope to a tree or pipe while putting little strain on the rope. It is an easy anchor knot, but tension must remain on the knot, or it will slip. This can be remedied by making another loop around the object and under the center of the clove hitch.

• **Taut-Line Hitch**:

The taut-line hitch is an adjustable loop knot for use on lines under tension, useful when the length of a line will need to be periodically adjusted in order to maintain tension.

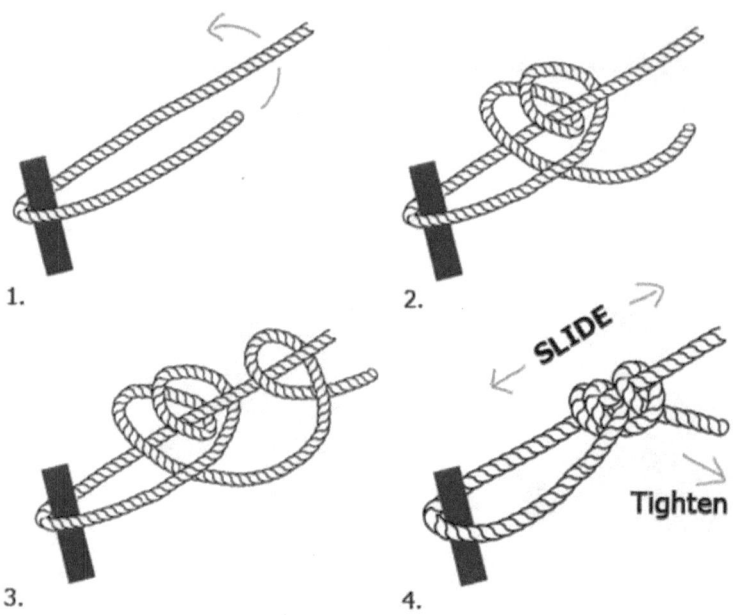

Figure 5-15: Taut-Line Hitch.

This knot is tied by tying a rolling hitch around the standing part after passing around an anchor object. Tension is maintained by sliding the hitch to adjust the size of the loop, thus changing the effective length of the standing part without retying the knot. It is typically used for securing tent lines, for tying down aircraft, for creating adjustable moorings in tidal areas, and to secure loads on vehicles.

• **Sheet Bend, Double Sheet Bend**:

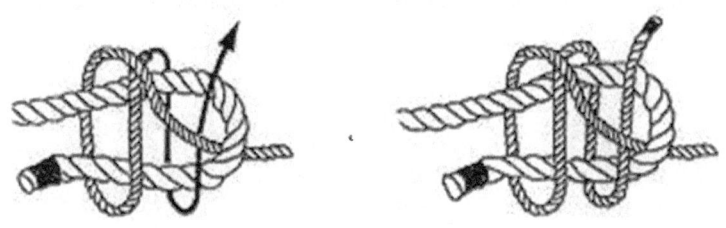

Figure 5-16: Sheet Bend, Double Sheet Bend.

This knot is used to tie together the ends of two ropes of equal or unequal diameter. It will also join wet rope and will not slip or draw tight under load. It can be used to tie the ends of several ropes to the end of one rope. When a single rope is tied to multiple ropes, the bight is formed with the multiple of ropes.

• **Prusik, End-of-Line and Center-of-Line**:

Figure 5-17: Prusik, End-of-Line

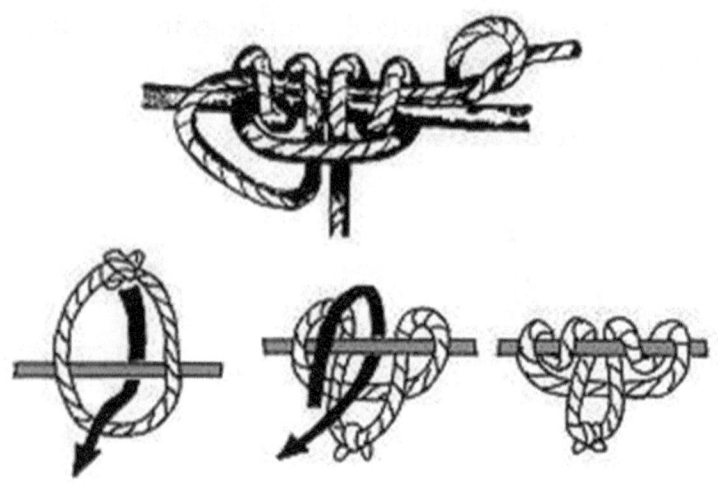

Figure 5-17A: Prusik, Center –of-Line.

This knot ties a short rope around a longer rope (for example, a sling rope around a climbing rope) in such a manner that the short rope will slide on the climbing rope if no tension is applied and will hold if tension is applied on the short rope. This knot can be tied with an end of rope or bight of rope. When tied with an end of rope, the knot is finished off with a bowline for safety:

Figure 5-17B: Prusik with Bowline.

The nonslip nature of the knot on another rope allows climbing of ropes with foot holds. It can also be used to anchor ropes or the end of a traction splint on a branch or ski pole.

• **Bowline**:

Figure 5-18: Bowline.

Around-the-body bowline is a basic knot used to provide a loop which will not slip nor tighten up under strain. The bowline is finished with an overhand knot.

There are many variants of this knot, to include double loop bowline, and bowline on a bight. The bowline has been replaced by the figure 8 in most climbing or rescue applications as the figure 8 does not weaken the rope as much.

- **Figure-8 Knot, Figure-8-on-a-Bight, and Retraceable Figure-8**:

Figure 5-19: Figure-8 Knot.

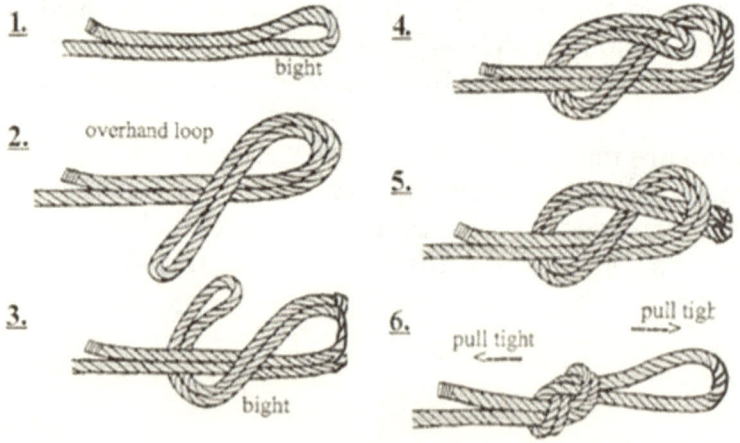

Figure 5-20: Figure-8-on-a-Bight.

The Figure 8 knot is the main rescue knot in use today. It has the advantage of being stronger than the bowline and is easier to tie and check. It's one disadvantage is that when wet, it may be more difficult to untie than the bowline after being stressed. The figure 8 (or figure-of-eight) can be used as an anchor knot on fixed ropes.

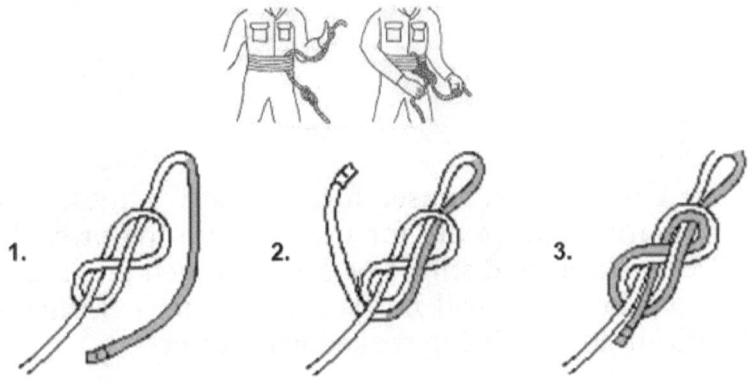

Figure 5-21: Retraceable Figure-8.

• **Sheepshank**:

Figure 5-22: Sheepshank.

The sheepshank is used to shorten a rope or take up slack. The sheepshank knot is not stable; it will fall apart under too much load or too little load.

• Carrick Bend:

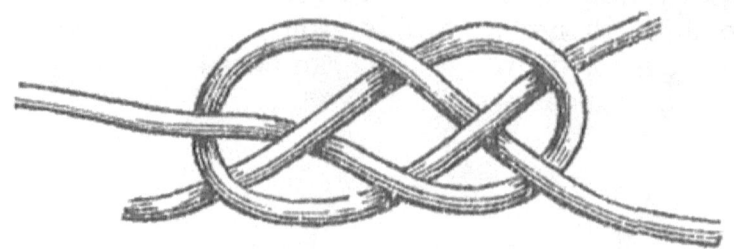

Figure 5-23: Carrick Bend.

The Carrick bend is used for joining two lines. It is particularly appropriate for very heavy rope or cable that is too large and stiff to be easily formed into other common bends. It will not jam even after carrying a significant load or being soaked with water.

II. Lashings

Lashings are used to hold two or more poles together, a form of primitive construction. Lashings are to build structures like shelters, tripods and drying racks.

• Square Lashing:

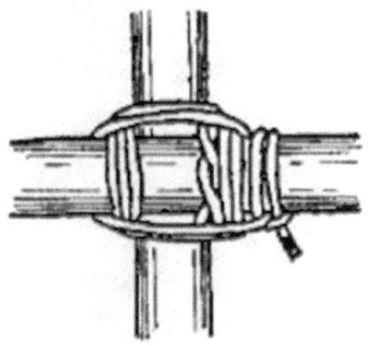

Figure 5-24: Square Lashing.

A square lashing begins and ends with a clove hitch and binds poles at a 90° angle. It is stronger than the diagonal lashing, but the square lashing cannot be used if a gap exists between poles. To make a square lashing, start with a clove hitch around one pole. Twist short end around long and wrap the rope around both poles, alternately going over and under each pole about three or four turns. Tighten the lashing by surrounding it with three or four frapping turns. Finish with two or three tight half hitches.

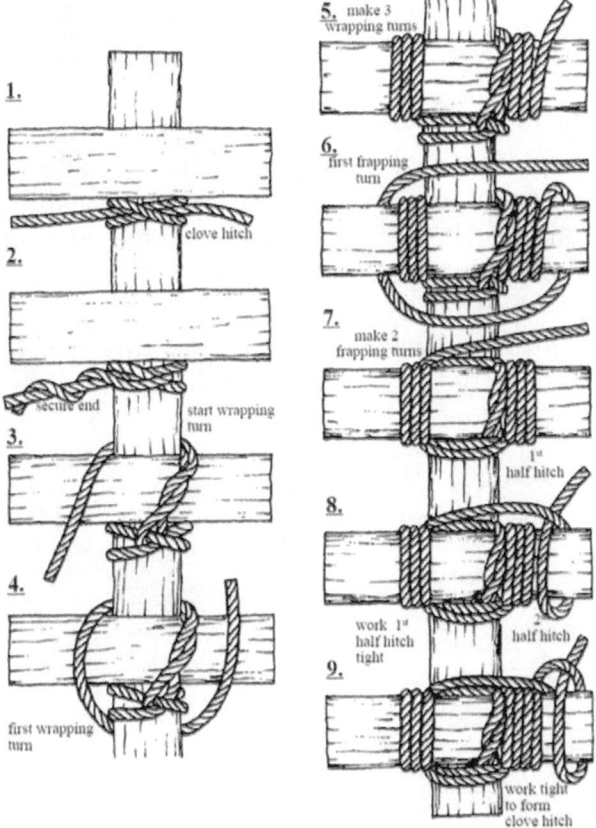

Figure 5-25: How to make a Square Lashing.

83

• Diagonal Lashing

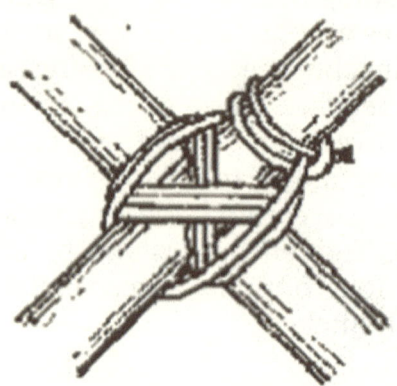

Figure 5-26: Diagonal Lashing.

This lashing binds poles that cross each other at a 45° to 90° angle. Cross bracing at 90° is only used if a gap exists between poles. To make a diagonal lashing, start with a single timber hitch (see below) around both poles. Wrap three or four turns around the two poles in one axis followed by three or four turns in the other axis. Tighten the lashing by surrounding it with three or four frapping turns. Finish with a clove hitch.

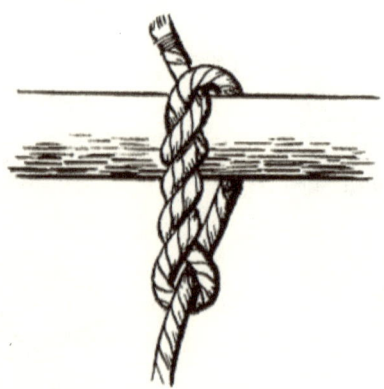

Figure 5-27: Timber Hitch.

• Shear Lashing

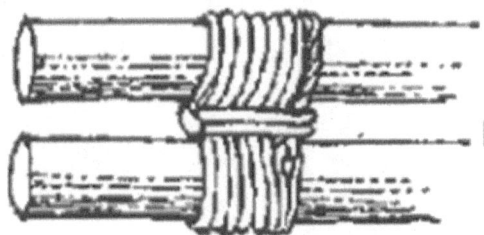

Figure 5-28: Shear Lashing.

A shear lashing begins and ends with a clove hitch and binds poles at a 0° to 45° angle. Use this when poles must flexibly swing apart in a scissors motion such as the shear legs of an A-frame.

• Tripod Lashing

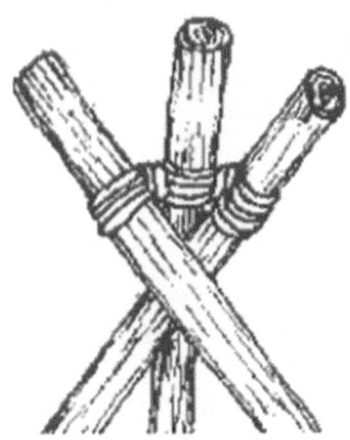

Figure 5-29: Tripod Lashing.

A tripod lashing begins and ends with a clove hitch and binds poles to be arranged to form a pyramid. Use this to hang a pot above a fire or as the basis for a strong, steady structure.

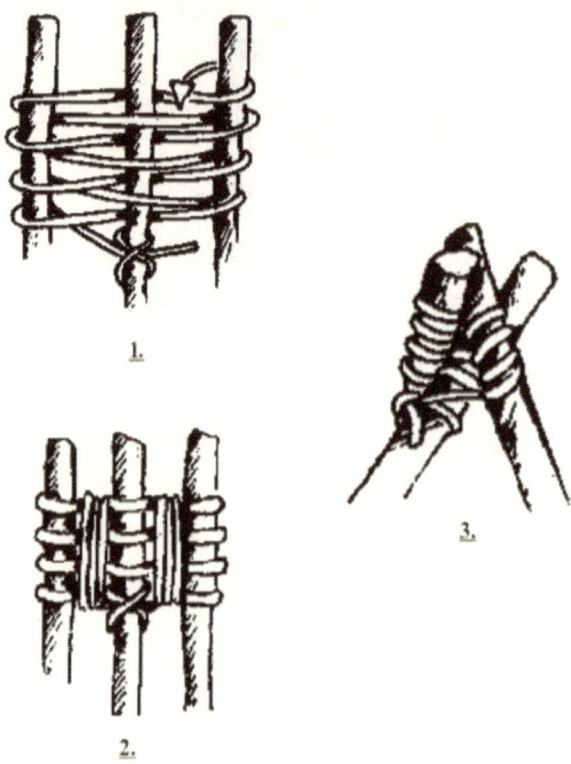

Figure 5-30: How to make a Tripod Lashing.

To make a tripod lashing, start with a clove hitch around one pole. Wrap about six racking turns around the three poles weaving in and out between them. Make two or three tight frapping turns in the two gaps. Finish with a clove hitch. Cross the two outside poles to form the tripod.

6

Food and Water

A. Water.

Water is one of the three top requirements in a survival situation, second only to shelter. More than three-fourths of our bodies are composed of fluids. The human body loses fluid due of heat, cold, stress, and exertion. To function effectively, we must replace the fluid our bodies lose.

Vital skills in any survival situation regarding water include the ability to:

• PROCURE water
• PREPARE (i.e. filter and purify) water, to be able to
• STORE and/or TRANSPORT water

I. Water Requirements:

The average adult requires 2 to 3 quarts (1 to 3 liters) of water daily. Water requirements increase with exposure to heat, exposure to cold, exercise or strenuous work, high altitudes, burns, illness and digestion.

A normal human cannot live much longer than three days without water. This is true not only in hot areas where one loses water rapidly through perspiration, but also in cold areas where the body actually loses more fluid from respiration (breathing) than in hot climates.

Cold weather also affects the body's ability to detect thirst; most people drink significantly less water when it's cold. Urine output also tends to increase as the cold moves blood and other bodily fluids from your arms and legs to your core, further leading to dehydration.

II. Water Procurement

Naturally occurring water sources include surface water such as lakes, rivers and streams. Water commonly collects in drainage areas, such as the low areas of valleys and draws. Subsurface water sources are indicated by dry lake beds and dry creek beds (wadis).

Figure 6-1: Dry Riverbed, or Wadi.

To find water in the desert, all trails lead to water. Follow trails in the direction of which the trails converge. Signs of camps, campfire ashes, animal droppings and trampled terrain may mark trails.

Figure 6-1: Indicators of Water in the Desert.

Figure 6-2: Indicators of Water in the Desert.

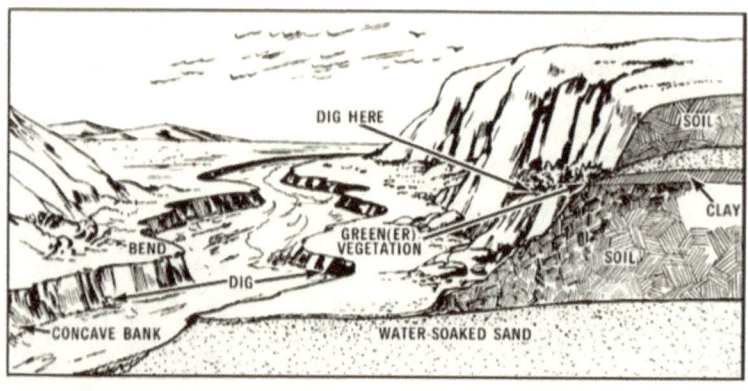

Figure 6-3: Water Indicators in the Desert.

Look for hollows, canyons, and caves at the base of mountains.

Indicators of the presence of water include animal activity. All living things need water; animal tracks, birds and flying insects indicate the presence of water. Grazing animals, such as deer, are usually never far from water and usually drink at dawn and dusk. Converging game trails often lead to water. Carnivores (meat eaters) are not reliable indicators of water. They get moisture from the animals they eat and can go without water for long periods.

Birds can lead you to water; they drink at dawn and dusk. In the desert, a group of birds flying in one direction – especially around sundown - are flying towards water. Their flight during these times is usually fast and low to ground. Bird tracks or chirping sounds in the evening or early morning sometimes indicates that water is nearby. Do not rely on water birds to lead to water; they fly long distances without stopping.

Insects, especially bees, are good indicators of water. Bees will usually have a water source within range of their nests or hives. Most flies stay within 100 meters (330 feet) of water. Ants need water. A column of ants marching up a tree is going to a small reservoir of trapped water; such reservoirs can be found even in arid areas - you can stuff cloth in the hole to absorb the water and then wring it from the cloth.

Human tracks will usually lead to a well, bore hole, or soak. Scrub or rocks may cover it to reduce evaporation. Replace the cover after use.

Water can also be found in the cracks of rocks in mountains – look for clusters of bird droppings, this indicates where birds go for water. A technique to extract water from deep cracks is to use a cloth and feed it down into the crack to extract the water.

Figure 6-4: Water found in the base of rocky hills and mountains.

The following table lists possible sources of water in various environments:

Environ-ment	Sources of Water	Means of Obtaining and/or making Potable	Remarks
Frigid Areas	Snow and Ice	Melt and Purify	Do not eat without melting! Snow & ice are no purer than the water they came from. Sea ice that is gray is salty. Do not use it without desalting it. Sea ice that is crystalline with a bluish tint has very little salt in it.
At Sea	Sea	Use Desalinator	Do not drink seawater without desalinating.
	Rain	Catch rain in tarps or other water-holding containers	If tarp or water-holding material is coated in salt, wash it in the sea before use - very little salt will remain.
	Sea Ice		(see previous remarks for Frigid Areas)
Beach	Ground	Dig hole deep enough to allow water to seep in; obtain rocks, buld fire & heat rocks, drop hot rocks in water; hold cloth over water to absorb steam, wring water from cloth.	Alternate method if a suitable container is available. Fill container with seawater, build fire & heat rocks, drop hot rocks in water; hold cloth over water to absorb steam, wring water from cloth.

Figure 6-5: Water Sources in Different Environments.

Environment	Sources of Water	Means of Obtaining and/or making Potable	Remarks
Beach (cont'd)	Fresh	Digging behind first pressure ridge (first line of sand dunes) will allow collection of fresh water.	
Desert	Ground	Dig holes deep enough to allow water to seep into.	In a sand dune belt, any available water will be found beneath the original valley floor at the edge of the dunes.
	In valleys and low areas.		
	At foot of concave banks of dry riverbeds.		
	At foot of cliffs or rocky outcrops.		
	At first depression behind first sand dune of dry lakes.		
	Presence damp surface sand.		
	Presence of green vegetation.		

Figure 6-6 (continued): Water Sources in Different Environments.

Environment	Sources of Water	Means of Obtaining and/or making Potable	Remarks
Desert (cont'd)	Cacti	Cut off the top of a barrel cactus and mash or squeeze the pulp. CAUTION: do not eat the pulp. Place pulp in mouth, suck out the juice and discard pulp.	Without a machete, cutting into a cactus is difficult and takes time, since you must get past the long, strong spines and the tough rind.
	Depressions or holes in rocks		Periodic rainfall may collect in pools, seep into fissures, or collect in holes in rocks.
	Fissures in rocks		
	Porous rock		
	Condensation on metal	Use cloth to absorb water, then wring water from cloth.	Extreme temperature variations between night and day may cause condensation on metal surfaces.

Figure 6-7 (continued): Water Sources in Different
Environments.

Heavy dew can provide water. Tie rags or tufts of fine grass around your ankles and walk-through dew-covered grass before sunrise. As the rags or grass tufts absorb the dew, wring the water into a container. Repeat the process until you have a supply of water or until the dew is gone. Australian natives sometimes mop up as much as 1 liter an hour this way.

Fluid	Remarks
Alcoholic Beverages	Dehydrates the body and clouds judgment.
Urine	Contains harmful body wastes, is about 2% salt.
Blood	Is salty and considered a food, therefore requires additional body fluids to digest. May transmit disease.
Seawater	Is about 4% salt. It takes about 2 liters of body fluids to rid the body of waste from 1 liter of seawater. Therefore, by drinking seawater, you deplete your body's water supply, which can cause death.

Figure 6-8: The Effects of Substitute Fluids.

Other water sources are water vines and water trees. Water sometimes gathers in the crotches of trees or rock crevices. You can use a tube or stuff a cloth in the hole to absorb the water and then wring it from the cloth.

Green bamboo thickets are an excellent source of fresh water. Water from green bamboo is clear and odorless. To get the water, bend a green bamboo stalk, tie it down, and cut off the top. The water will drip freely during the night. Old, cracked bamboo may also contain water.

CAUTION: purify the water before drinking it.

Figure 6-9: Water from Green Bamboo.

Wherever you find banana trees, plantain trees, or sugarcane, you can get water. Cut down the tree, leaving about a 30-centimeter (12-inch) stump, and scoop out the center of the stump so that the hollow is bowl-shaped. Water from the roots will immediately start to fill the hollow. The first three fillings of water will be bitter but succeeding fillings will be palatable. The stump will supply water for up to 4 days. Be sure to cover it to keep out insects.

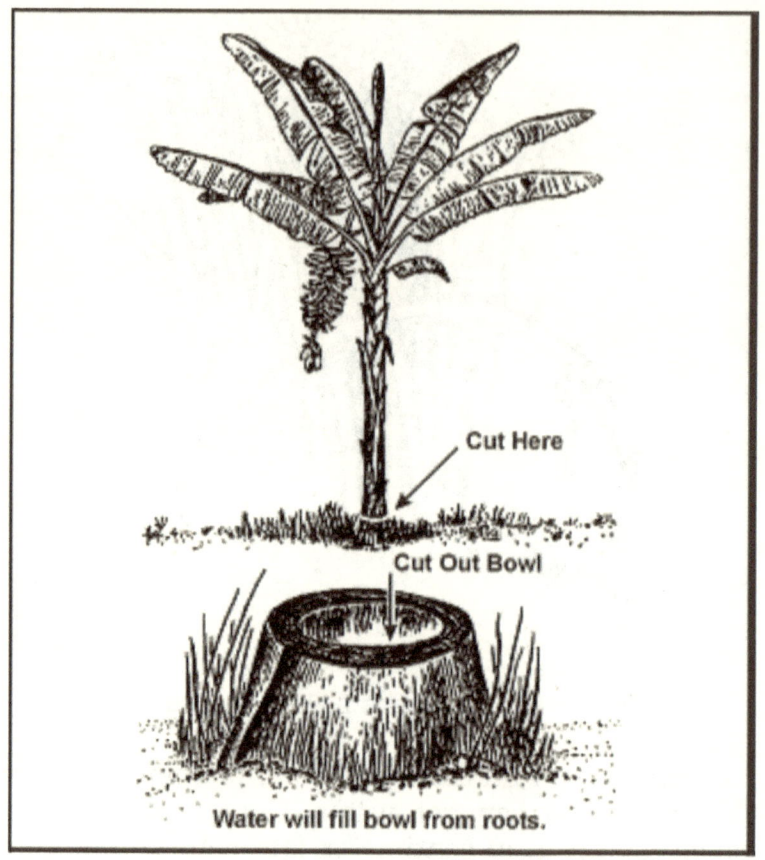

Figure 6-10: Water from Plantain or Banana Tree Stump.

Some tropical vines can give you water. Cut a notch in the vine as high as you can reach, then cut the vine off close to the ground. Catch the dropping liquid in a container or in your mouth.

Figure 6-11: Water Vines – Sri Lanka.

CAUTION: Do not drink the liquid if it is sticky, milky, or bitter tasting.

The milk from young, green (unripe) coconuts is a good thirst quencher. However, the milk from mature, brown, coconuts contain an oil that acts as a laxative. Drink in moderation only.

In the tropics you may find large trees whose branches support air plants. These air plants may hold a considerable amount of rainwater in their overlapping, thickly growing leaves. Strain the water through a cloth to remove insects and debris.

You can get water from plants with moist pulpy centers. Cut off a section of the plant and squeeze or smash the pulp so that the moisture runs out. Catch the liquid in a container.

Plant roots may provide water. Dig or pry the roots out of the ground, cut them into short pieces, and smash the pulp so that the moisture runs out. Catch the liquid in a container. Fleshy leaves, stems, or stalks, such as bamboo, contain water. Cut or notch the stalks at the base of a joint to drain out the liquid.

The following trees can also provide water:

• Palms. The buri, coconut, sugar, rattan, and nips contain liquid. Bruise a lower frond and pull it down so the tree will "bleed" at the injury.

• Traveler's tree. Found in Madagascar, this tree has a cuplike sheath at the base of its leaves in which water collects.

• Umbrella tree. The leaf bases and roots of this tree of western tropical Africa can provide water.

• Baobab tree. This tree of the sandy plains of northern Australia and Africa collects water in its bottlelike trunk during the wet season. Frequently, you can find clear, fresh water in these trees after weeks of dry weather.

CAUTION: Do not keep the sap from plants longer than 24 hours. It begins fermenting, becoming dangerous as a water source.

Water Distillation

Other water sources are transpiration bags and solar stills. Stills draw moisture from the ground and from plant material. They can be used in various areas of the world, including arid or desert areas. Depending on the environment, a still takes about 24 hours to produce 0.5 to 1 quart (0.5 to 1 liter) of water.

Water from these sources may have the taste and color of a dark tea, which does not require filtration or purification, but may require purification if stored over time.

There are two types of above ground stills; vegetation bag still and transpiration bag still.

Vegetation Bag Still: this requires a sunny slope on which to place the still, a clear plastic bag, green leafy vegetation, and a small rock.

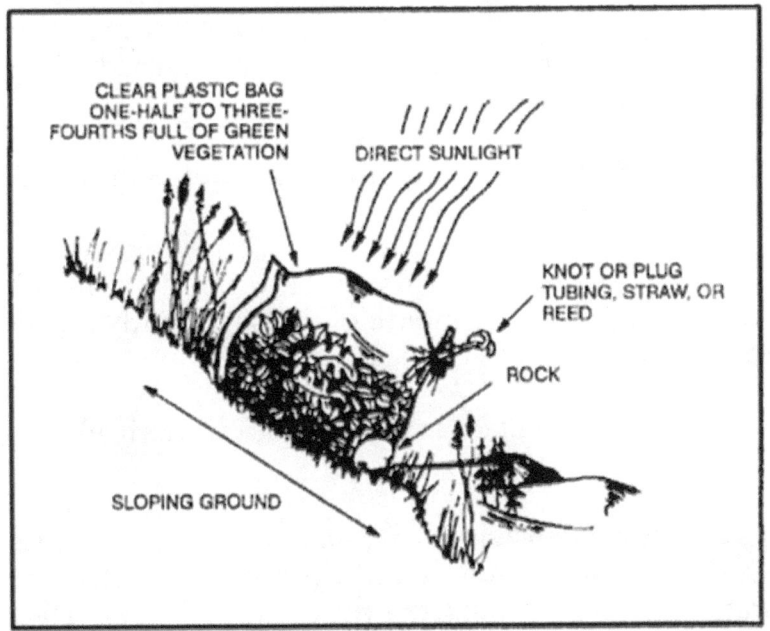

Figure 6-11: Vegetation Bag Still

To make the vegetation bag still:

• Fill the bag with air by turning the opening into the breeze or by "scooping" air into the bag.

• Fill the plastic bag one-half to three-fourths full of green leafy vegetation. Be sure to remove all hard sticks or sharp spines that might puncture the bag.

• Place a small rock or similar item in the bag.

• Close the bag and tie the mouth securely as close to the end of the bag as possible to keep the maximum amount of air space. If you have a piece of tubing, a small straw, or a hollow reed, insert one end in the mouth of the bag before you tie it securely. Then tie off or plug the tubing so that air will not escape. This tubing will allow you to drain out condensed water without untying the bag.

CAUTION: Do not use poisonous vegetation; it will provide poisonous liquid.

• Place the bag, mouth downhill, on a slope in full sunlight. Position the mouth of the bag slightly higher than the low point in the bag.

• Settle the bag in place so that the rock works itself into the low point in the bag.

To get the condensed water from the still, loosen the tie around the bag's mouth and tip the bag so that the water collected around the rock will drain out. Then retie the mouth securely and reposition the still to allow further condensation.

Change the vegetation in the bag after extracting most of the water from it. This will ensure maximum output of water.

Transpiration Bag Still: this is similar to the vegetation bag, only easier. Simply tie the plastic bag over a leafy tree limb with a tube inserted and tie the mouth of the bag off tightly around the branch to form an airtight seal. Tie the end of the limb so that it hangs below the level of the mouth of the bag. The water will collect there.

The same limb may be used for 3 to 5 days without causing long-term harm to the limb. It will heal itself within a few hours of removing the bag.

Figure 6-12: Water Transpiration Bag

Solar Still: This is a below-ground still that works on the same principles as the two previously described above-ground stills.

Select a site where you believe the soil will contain moisture (such as a dry streambed or a low spot where rainwater has collected). The soil at this site should be easy to dig, and sunlight must hit the site most of the day. To construct a solar still, you need a digging tool, a container, a clear plastic sheet, a drinking tube, and a rock.

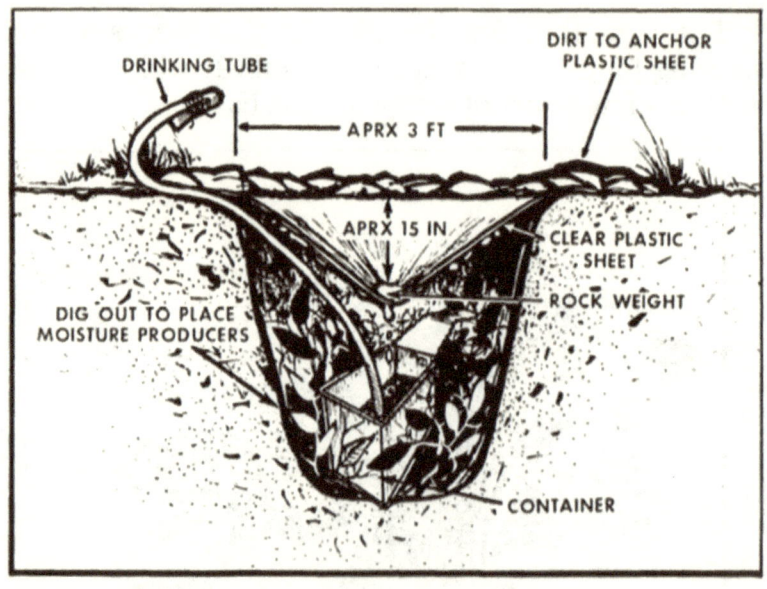

Figure 6-13: Solar Still

• Dig a bowl-shaped hole about 1 meter (3 feet) across and 60 centimeters (24 inches) deep.

• Dig a sump in the center of the hole. The sump's depth and perimeter will depend on the size of the container that you have to place in it. The bottom of the sump should allow the container to stand upright.

• Anchor the tubing to the container's bottom by forming a loose overhand knot in the tubing.

• Place the container upright in the sump.

• Extend the unanchored end of the tubing up, over, and beyond the lip of the hole.

• Place the plastic sheet over the hole, covering its edges with soil to hold it in place.

• Place a rock in the center of the plastic sheet.

• Lower the plastic sheet into the hole until it is about 40 centimeters (16 inches) below ground level. It now forms an inverted cone with the rock at its apex. Make sure that the cone's apex is directly over your container. Also make sure the plastic cone does not touch the sides of the hole because the earth will absorb the condensed water.

• Put more soil on the edges of the plastic to hold it securely in place and to prevent the loss of moisture.

• Plug the tube when not in use to keep the moisture from evaporating and to keep insects out.

You can drink water without disturbing the still by using the tube as a straw. By opening the still, you release the moist, warm air that has accumulated.

You may want to use plants in the hole as a moisture source. If so, dig out additional soil from the sides of the hole to form a slope on which to place the plants. Then proceed as above.

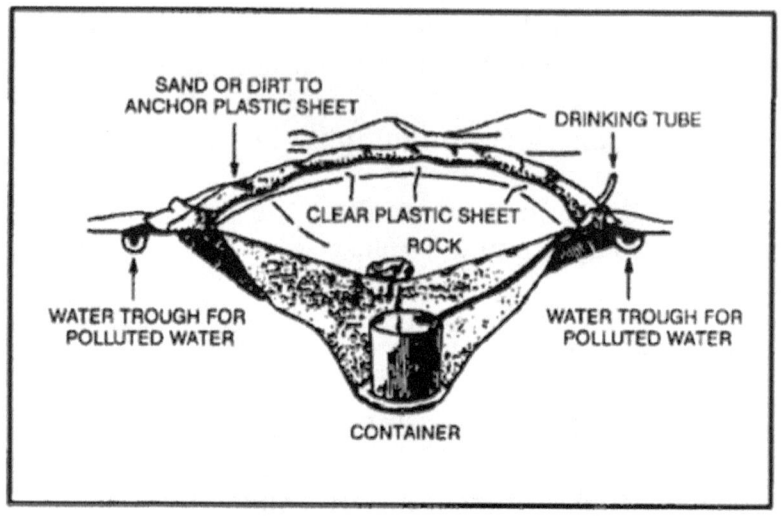

Figure 6-14: Solar Still

A similar solar still can be used to produce clean water if polluted water is your only moisture source (see figure 6-14 above).

Dig a small trough outside the hole about 10 inches (25 centimeters) from the still's lip. Dig the trough about 25 centimeters (10 inches) deep and 8 centimeters (3 inches) wide. Pour the polluted water in the trough.

Be sure you do not spill any polluted water around the rim of the hole where the plastic sheet touches the soil. The trough holds the polluted water, and the soil filters it as the still draws it. The water then condenses on the plastic and drains into the container. This process works extremely well when your only water source is salt water.

You will need at least three stills to meet your individual daily water intake needs. In comparison to the belowground still and the water transpiration bag still, the vegetation bag produces the best yield of water.

III. Water Filtration

The basic process of filtering water in a survival situation is to remove debris such as sediment or debris from the water.

CAUTION: Filtration removes large particles from water, but FILTRATION DOES NOT PURIFY WATER.

Water Filtration Devices

If the water you find is muddy, stagnant, and foul-smelling, you can clear the water —

• By placing it in a container and letting it stand for 12 hours.

• By pouring it through a filtering system.

There are many commercially available water filtration systems for outdoors enthusiasts and for residential or installation purposes.

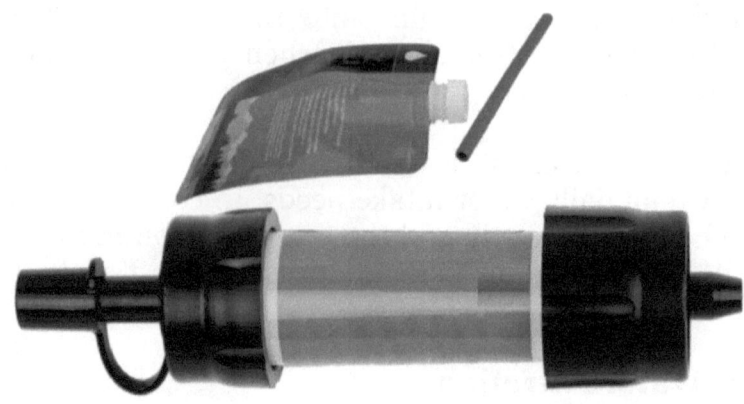

Figure 6-15: Commercially available water filtration systems.

Improvised water filters can be fabricated out of plastic bottles or bamboo tubes, or cloth with several layers of filtering material such as sand, crushed rock, charcoal:

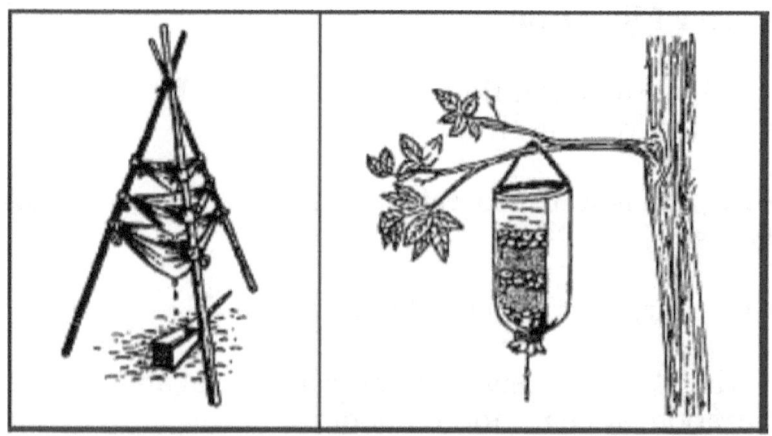

Figure 6-16: Improvised Water Filtering Systems

Figure 6-17: Improvised Water Filter System: 2 Jars + strip of Gauze.

Remove the odor from water by adding charcoal from your fire. Charcoal is also helpful in absorbing some agricultural and industrial chemicals. Let the water stand for 45 minutes before drinking it.

IV. Water Purification

Water purification kills bacteria, viruses, and parasites that cause water borne diseases.

Potentially fatal waterborne illnesses may be contracted by drinking non-potable water. Two of the most prevalent pathogens found in most water sources throughout the world are:

• Giardia, which causes Giardiasis (beaver fever), characterized by an explosive, watery diarrhea accompanied by severe cramps lasting 7 to 14 days.

• Cryptosporidium, which causes Cryptosporidiosis. It is much like Giardiasis, only more severe and prolonged, and there is no known cure but time. Diarrhea may be mild and can last from 3 days to 2 weeks.

NOTE: The only effective means of neutralizing Cryptosporidium is by boiling or by using a commercial micro-filter or reverse-osmosis filtration system.

Chemical disinfectants such as iodine tablets or bleach have not shown to be 100 percent effective in eliminating Cryptosporidium.
Other diseases or organisms are:

• Dysentery. Symptoms include severe, prolonged diarrhea with bloody stools, fever, and weakness.

• Cholera and typhoid (one may be susceptible to these diseases regardless of inoculations). Cholera can cause profuse, watery diarrhea, vomiting, and leg cramps.

Typhoid symptoms include fever, headache, loss of appetite, constipation, and bleeding in the bowel.

• Hepatitis A. Symptoms include diarrhea, abdominal pain, jaundice, and dark urine. This infection can spread through close person-to-person contact or ingestion of contaminated water or food.

• Flukes. Stagnant, polluted water, especially in tropical areas, often contains blood flukes. If you swallow flukes, they will bore into the bloodstream, live as parasites, and cause disease.

• Leeches. If you swallow a leech, it can hook onto the throat passage or inside the nose. It will suck blood, create a wound, and move to another area. Each bleeding wound may become infected.

Rainwater collected in clean containers or in plants is usually safe for drinking. However, purify water from lakes, ponds, swamps, springs, or streams, especially the water near human settlements or in the tropics.

When possible, purify all water you get from vegetation or from the ground by the methods described below.

Water Purification Methods include:

• Boiling: this is the safest method of purifying your drinking water. Water brought to a rolling boil for at least one minute will destroy all living waterborne pathogens. Altitude affects the heat transfer, so in alpine environments, boil water for at least three minutes.

• Solar Disinfection (SODIS): Solar water disinfection is a simple process that uses ultra-violet light (UV) from the sun's rays to effectively rid water of disease-causing biological substances such as bacteria, viruses, and protozoa; the UV light slices through organisms and destroys their cell membranes and DNA.

Additionally, when UV rays strike dissolved oxygen molecules in the water, natural free radicals are created that tear apart microorganisms. Finally, UV energy creates heat. This heat creates a pasteurization effect on the microorganisms; microbes don't stand a chance.

Fill plastic drink bottles with low-turbidity water, shake them to oxygenate, and place the bottles out for 6 hours if sunny, or 2 days if cloudy. (The maximum recommended diameter of a SODIS bottle is 4" or the UV-A rays will not kill all the bacteria).

NOTE: only use clear glass or plastic bottles or bags for the SODIS method. Tinted glass or plastic (blue, green, etc.) will prevent UV rays from going through the water.

Figure 6-18: Solar Disinfection of Water (SODIS)

• Chemical: purifying water for drinking using chemical methods includes the use of water purification tablets, tincture of iodine, chlorine tablets and/or laundry bleach, and potassium permanganate crystals.

Chemical purification of water instructions:

• Water purification tablets (follow the directions provided).

• Tincture of iodine: place 5 drops of 2 percent in a container such as a canteen or water bottle full of clear water. If the canteen is full of cloudy or cold water, use 10 drops. (Let the canteen of water stand for 30 minutes before drinking.)

• Use 2 drops of 10 percent (military strength) povidone-iodine or 1 percent titrated povidone iodine. The civilian equivalent is usually 2 percent strength, so 10 drops may be needed. Let stand for 30 minutes. If the water is cold and clear, wait 60 minutes. If it's very cold or cloudy, add 4 drops and wait 60 minutes.

• Place 2 drops of chlorine bleach (5.25 percent sodium hypochlorite) in a canteen of water. Let stand 30 minutes. If the water is cold or cloudy, wait 60 minutes. Remember that not all laundry bleach is the same around the world; check the available level of sodium hypochlorite.

• Potassium permanganate (commonly marketed as Condy's Crystals) can be used for a number of applications, including emergency disinfection of water. The crystals are of a non-uniform size, so you must judge the actual dosage by the color of the water after adding the crystals. Add three small crystals to 1 liter (1 quart) of water. If the water turns a bright pink after waiting 30 minutes, the water is considered purified.

If the water turns a dark pink, there is too much potassium permanganate to drink safely. Either add more water to dilute the mixture or save it for use as an antiseptic solution. If the water becomes a full red, like the color of cranberry juice, the solution may be used as an antifungal solution.

NOTE: After purifying water using chemical methods in a container such as a canteen or water bottle, you must partially unscrew the cap and turn the container upside down to rinse unpurified water from the threads of the neck of the container where your mouth touches.

V. Water Storage Containers

Figure 6-19: Metal water container for purification by boiling over fire.

Figure 6-20: Improvised bamboo water containers.

How to boil water in bamboo without placing the container over a fire:

Figure 6-21: Bamboo Water Boiler with Stones.

1. Fill the Boiler with water, place the stones in the fire.

2. Place hot stones into the water, the water will boil.

B. FOOD

Survival concerns regarding food includes the ability to PROCURE, PREPARE, and to be able to STORE and TRANSPORT food in a survival situation. While it is true that a human can live up to three or four weeks without food, the average adult requires 2000 calories a day, for normal daily activities and one will be more efficient and alert and have more confidence if able to satisfy hunger.

Short term survival food requirement can be met with canned foods; it makes sense to carry some high-energy food in your survival kit. Dried, dehydrated or otherwise preserved and packaged foods such as military rations or foods found in outdoor stores.

Canned meat products (such as Spam® or corned beef) are remarkable survival foods; in extreme circumstances, four people could live off of one can of SPAM® for three to four days. Disadvantage of canned foods is weight and volume; disadvantage of dried or dehydrated foods is they require water to prepare.

If you have dehydrated or canned food, or military rations, try to stretch them out as far as possible; you do not know how long your survival situation is going to last! Supplement your food supply from the start with any wild foods discussed below.

This offers the double advantage of gradually becoming accustomed to the "wild" diet and extending your food supplies. Always keep an eye out for edible plants that can be carried in your rucksack or in your pockets for later cooking and eating.

When living off the land, be prepared to eat anything and everything. Old prejudices or taboos should be put aside, and a survival mindset maintained, for the absolute requirement of getting food somehow to keep going. All objections to wholesome food are hysteria.

For example, one may enjoy eating live oysters – a delicacy – but may recoil in horror at the thought of eating raw snails, although raw snails are just as good food, just as tasty, and are in fact cleaner feeders than oysters as they live on wholesome foliage.

I. Animals

With very few exceptions, almost all animals can be eaten raw, however the process of cooking kills bacteria, viruses and parasites. In areas where rabies is prevalent (Asia, Africa, rural areas in the United States), the meat of mammals must be thoroughly cooked and precautions must be taken against fluid transfers while preparing the meat.

The suggested method for cooking meat (or plants) for survival purposes is to boil into a soup or a stew; this way all the nutrients are saved within your cooking vessel. Owing to their high food value when compared with most vegetable foods, small animals (just two or three snails, or some frog's legs) are worth collecting for adding to a meal of boiled leaves or roots. Finding animal food in quantity is uncertain, whereas vegetable food – especially wild plants – is generally plentiful.

To skin and clean small game, cut off the head, make a small incision just skin deep down the center of the breast and abdomen, then pull the skin off the back from the top downwards. Afterwards cut open the lower abdomen and remove the organs.

• **Rats & Mice**: both are palatable meat, the taste is comparable to chicken. Skin the animal and clean out the internal organs and boil them; about ten minutes for rat, five minutes for mice. Either can be cooked with dandelion leaves for a stew. Be sure to include the livers.

• **Birds**: all birds are edible. Waterfowl may be tough and unpalatable but are nonetheless good nutrition.

• **Dogs and Cats**: providing so much food, they are worth some trouble in capture by friendly advances. Either animal stewed with edible leaves is an excellent meal.

• **Snakes and Lizards**: cut off the heads, clean them and skin them. With poisonous snakes, chop off the head about three fingers width behind the head to prevent the poison sacs from potentially introducing poison into the meat. Boil for about ten minutes.

• **Hedgehogs**: these European mammals are commonly found in dry ditches. Turn them on their backs, tickle the body lightly with fingers or a stick. It will then poke out its head, which can be severed with the stroke of a knife. Skin and stew with edible leaves.

Catching Animals

Small birds and mice: a standard commercially available mousetrap can be effective. Conceal the trap by sprinkling short pieces of dry grass, baited with bread or biscuit crumbs for smaller birds; for larger birds a large live worm impaled on the trigger can be used. Anchor the trap to the ground with a piece of string or wire.

Figure 6-22: Simple Wire Loop Snares.

Loop snares and drag snares are simple traps that can be fabricated from wire, which may be found in wrecked vehicles, etcetera. Rabbits and rats may be captured by snares set in the runs. A squirrel pole consists of many wire loop snares festooned upon a pole, which is placed leaning against a tree where squirrels have been observed. Squirrel poles are so effective that they are illegal in the United States.

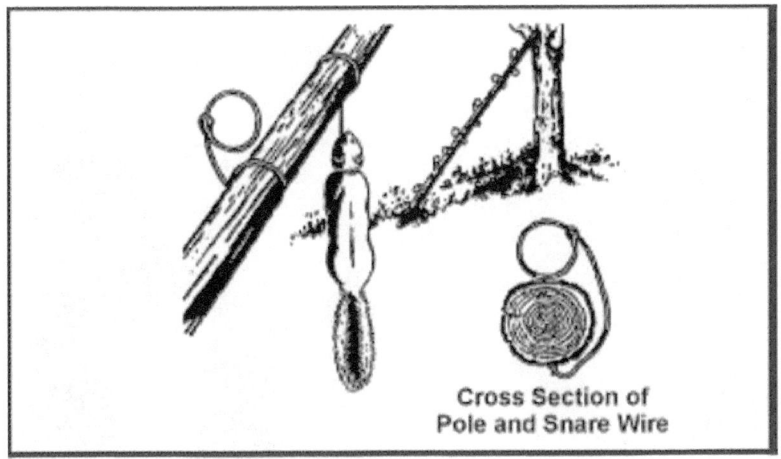

Cross Section of
Pole and Snare Wire

Figure 6-23: Squirrel Pole.

Fish spears or frog gigs can be fabricated from wood, bamboo or even using heavy wire such as coat hangers fastened to a shaft. Wood or bamboo can be hardened using fire.

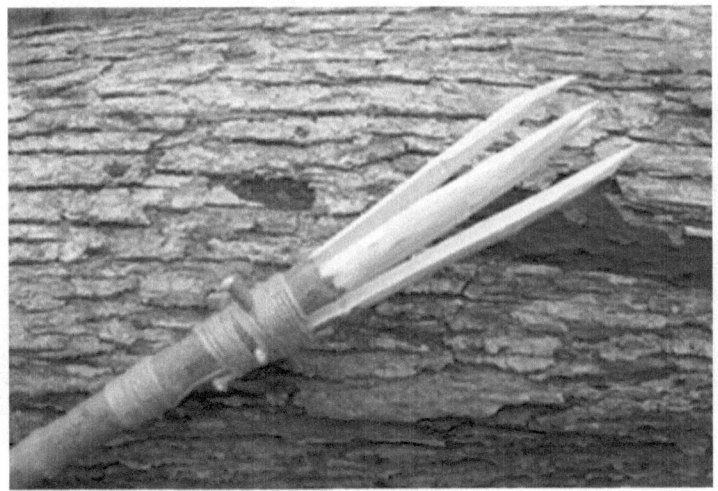

Figure 6-24: Fish Spear or Frog Gig.

Figure 6-25: Fish Traps using Sticks & Stones.

Successful hunting, trapping fish and game is a difficult, energy-consuming enterprise. It is more likely, in a short-term survival situation, that you will be forced to resort to eating frogs, snails, slugs, worms and insects. The good news is that these creatures are plentiful, easy to harvest and are high in protein.

Frogs: The flesh of all frogs is tasty and wholesome, but most of the meat is found on the hind legs.

Snails: Snails are a real delicacy. Snails may be eaten in two ways; a) by cracking the shell and withdrawing the snail, and b) dropping them into boiling water for five minutes and pulling out the cooked snail with a pin.

Snails may be found by "combing" grassy fields with the fingers; they will be found on the stalks of the grass or on the ground. Standing hay is a rich finding ground for snails.

Slugs: An abundant food source for the warm, wet months of the year.

Slugs and snails are host to a potentially dangerous parasite; rat lungworm. If a human eats a raw snail or slug, these parasites will not live in the body but can produce a toxic reaction; 'eosinophilic meningitis'. To avoid this, slugs and snails must be cooked. Slugs and snails also eat things which are toxic to humans, therefore they must be prepared by cleaning, much like any animal. To gut a slug, kill it by chopping its head off then squeeze out the entrails. The slug will shrink considerably, and you will get slime on your hands.

Snails must be unshelled before performing this process; steam or roast the snail and remove it from the shell, then slit open the belly and remove the cooked entrails. Slugs and snails can be chopped up and cooked in a stew, or roasted over a fire.

Earthworms: Highly nutritious, earthworms often come out during heavy rains when the soil becomes saturated with water. Earthworms' bodies are filled with dirt, which can be removed by soaking them in water 3 to 24 hours or taking the worm in hand and squeezing the dirt out with your free fingers.

The flavor is a little bitter; frying worms until crispy offsets the squiggliness, drying reduces the sliminess, making them more palatable.

Ants: Most ant species are edible. Because ants secrete an acid when threatened, this gives them a vinegar-like flavor; pleasantly sour.

Ants can be roasted with salt. Ant larvae have no sour flavor; they can be found in clumps under rocks, or on top of anthills when they are being moved or kept warm.

To harvest ants, put a stick on an anthill, wait for it to get covered with ants, then shake it off into a container.

Grasshoppers and Crickets: Found in open meadows, grassland, fields and some forests, grasshoppers and crickets have a long tradition as human food. They are sold by in marketplaces all over Latin America, Asia and Africa. They are excellent fried or toasted, with oil and salt if available. The legs must be removed before eating as they will get stuck in the throat. They can also be dried and stored for future use.

Grasshoppers and crickets can be trapped in a glass jar using for bait a slice of apple, bread, carrot, lettuce, banana or stale beer, even.

Apply vaseline around the inside of the jar about two inches so the insects can't get out, then put the jar on its side on the ground in a grasshopper- or cricket-infested area, in the morning there will be some insects enjoying themselves in there. Put the lid on to suffocate them.

Termites: Termites can be harvested then toasted in a hot pan. They have a high oil content relative to the size of their body and are quite tasty with a slight nutty flavor. Winged termites (alates) are larger and fattier. In areas where the alates are plentiful, they are harvested using a lamp with netting; they are attracted to the light and will collect on the netting. At the right time of the year, a candle next to a mirror at dusk will attract these alates. Termites are also found in rotting wood.

Maggots: A traditional superfood, maggots are extremely fatty and a rich source of essential amino acids. Their ability to transform lean meat into essential fats is potentially lifesaving under certain conditions. Maggots can be fried in a pan or spread on bread or crackers like butter.

Aphids: Another edible insect, depending what foliage they are feeding on, aphids can range from slightly bitter to sweet. Simply collect aphids from infested plants and eat them fresh.

Sowbugs: Known as pill bugs or roly-polies, sowbugs are little gray pill shaped shrimp-like creatures found beneath rotten wood or rocks. They are tasty when toasted, although they can be eaten fresh.

Earwigs: Earwigs can be prepared the same as termites or sowbugs. They can be gathered by filling a low-sided can with a half-inch of vegetable oil (or other liquid, food-grade oil) and placing it on the ground; the earwigs will find their way in and drown. A beer bottle with a bit of stale beer in it will also attract earwigs.

Giant Water Bugs (lethocerus indicus): These enormous tropical beetles resemble large cockroaches but they are quite clean and quite edible. In Thailand they are known as "Maeng Da" (แมงดา) and are considered a delicacy. They are found in marshy areas, especially after heavy rains, and harvested with buckets or nets or by hand – take care to handle them from behind as their bite is quite painful. Steam them or fry them in oil, then crack the head off at the upper thorax and squeeze the innards out like squeezing toothpaste out of a tube. They taste like walnuts.

II. Plants

Owing to their relatively poor food value, larger quantities of plant stuffs must be eaten to obtain sufficient calories. On the other hand, owing to their high vitamin and other mineral value, edible leaves are very wholesome food and provide much bulk so that they satisfy the appetite. "Short commons" on this form of diet may result in better health and strength than an equal shortage of richer foods.

A considerable part of each day must be devoted to gathering and eating foliage if it has to be eaten raw. Animals who subsist on it spend the greater part of their waking hours eating, and the welfare of humans living on wild vegetation of a country will largely depend on the amount of time dedicated for this purpose, including the preparation as well as the consumption of the food.

Facing a survival situation therefore, every opportunity should be taken for collecting food, preparing it and eating it. An average cabbage, weighing one kilogram (or two pounds), if eaten raw cannot be chewed and swallowed in under half an hour, and nine cabbages would be required for proper nutrition.

Generally, it makes no difference if edible plants are cooked or eaten raw, but the advantage is that they can be ingested quickly. It is important to be able to recognize edible wild plants and have some idea as to which provide the best food, i.e. their nutritional value. Many, such as grasses, have minute nutritional value because their food material is encased in cellulose which humans cannot digest. But by searching in grassy fields, ditches etcetera, several nutritious plants may be found.

To learn more about edible and poisonous plants, make it a habit to identify five edible plants in your area, or in your destination area, and identify five toxic or poisonous plants. Some plants are common across vast regions, continents even. Some plants mimic others, so it is essential to be able to properly identify edible and toxic plants.

Stinging Nettles (urtica dioica): Originally native to Europe, much of temperate Asia and western North Africa, nettles are now found worldwide, including New Zealand and North America.

Figure 6-26: Stinging Nettles.

When young and bright green in color, nettles are a tasty and wholesome vegetable, rather like spinach. One minute boiling entirely removes the sting (older nettles require longer boiling), then boil for six minutes to prepare a soup. Stinging nettles have a very high nutritional value.

Clover (trifolium repens): not a grass, clover has a soft and rather fleshy leaf which can be chewed and swallowed rapidly. Most ordinary fields or pastures contain clumps of it. The food value is about the same as dandelion. It does not have the effect of stimulating the kidneys which is found in dandelion.

Figure 6-27: Clover - trifolium repens

Fiddlehead Ferns: The term 'fiddlehead ferns' is a general description of the unfurled new leaves of a fern, of any number of species. They vary in size, shape and edibility from species to species.

Fiddleheads are generally gathered in early springtime. They are also occasionally found in their prime for harvesting during the fall time in the Pacific Northwest region of the USA. The best time to collect varies from region to region, year to year and species to species. In the Pacific Northwest, the best time generally falls around the month of March.

Collect them when they are still tightly curled as they quickly become less palatable as they unfurl. Also, remove any of the brown, papery chaff from them outside. The most effective way to remove the chaff is by rubbing gently with the hands. Washing in cold water can also help.

Figure 6-28: Young Fiddlehead Ferns.

Fiddleheads should be cooked. Raw fiddleheads can carry foodborne illness and/or cause stomach upset if eaten in large quantities.

How to cook fiddleheads: rinse fiddleheads in several changes of cold water, removing any dirt or grit, before using. Fiddleheads are tasty steamed or sautéed. They can also be boiled for 6 to 8 minutes but avoid overcooking fiddleheads.

Bracken Fern (pteridium aquilinum): these ferns are noted for their large, highly divided leaves, bracken fern are probably the widest distribution of any fern in the world, found on all continents except Antarctica and in all environments except deserts, though their typical habitat is wetlands and shady areas in forest. The young curly fiddleheads shoots may be eaten lightly boiled, like asparagus. The roots of bracken are rich food but they must be dug down deep the get the whole root out; should be boiled till tender.

Figure 6-29: Bracken Fern - pteridium aquilinum.

CAUTION: Bracken fern contains the carcinogenic compound ptaquiloside, which some scientists believe may be linked to stomach cancer. The spores have also been implicated as carcinogens. However, ptaquiloside is water soluble, and is reduced by soaking bracken in cool water.

Korean and Japanese cooks traditionally soak the shoots in water and ash to detoxify the plant before eating. At boiling temperature, the carcinogen denatures almost completely. Salt and baking soda also help with volatilizing the chemical.

Sow Thistle (sonchus oleraceus): Flowering plants of the dandelion tribe within the sunflower family, sow thistles are annual, biennial or perennial herbs, with or without rhizomes and a few are even woody. Of all the edible wild plants - because of its plentiful occurrence worldwide - the sow thistle takes first place as a sustaining food.

It can be boiled (five to eight minutes boiling is ample), both the leaves and its thick succulent roots are delicacies. The fleshy part at the junction of leaves and root resembles the core of an artichoke. Eaten raw it is rather like lettuce, and the root is palatable.

Dandelion (taraxacum officinale and taraxacum erythrospermum): originally native to Eurasia and North America, the two species are now common worldwide. The food value of this well-known wildflower is high; the leaves are used for salads, and the roots may also be eaten.

Figure 6-30: Dandelion (taraxacum officinale and taraxacum erythrospermum).

Due to an alkaloid called taraxicin, this plant has an effect of the kidneys. If the leaves and roots are boiled for ten minutes and the water boiled away, some of the taraxicin will have gone and the bitter taste of the plant much reduced. Owing to the availability of this plant in large quantities and to its good food value, it must be regarded as one of the most important of the wild vegetable foods. The roots are at times very thick and fleshy. When many of the leaves are eaten raw, the palate becomes accustomed to the bitter taste which is then less noticeable. The stimulating effect upon the kidneys need cause no anxiety.

Arrowhead (sagittaria sagittifolia): This flowering plant, which forms large leaves, is native to wetlands across most of Europe from Ireland and Portugal to Finland and Bulgaria, and in Russia, Ukraine, Siberia, Japan, Turkey, China, Australia, Vietnam and the Caucasus. It is also cultivated as a food crop in some other countries. Arrowhead has a tuberous root like a potato and a white flower. Follow the rood down. The tuber is at its end. In China this plant is called "anti-famine herb".

Figure 6-31: Arrowhead (sagittaria sagittifolia).

Bladder wrack (fucus vesiculosus) seaweed: A seaweed found on the coasts of the North Sea, the western Baltic Sea, and the Atlantic and Pacific Oceans.

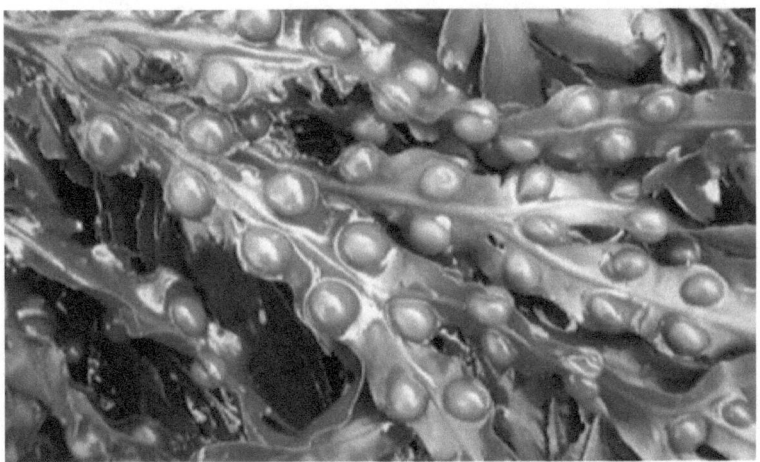

Figure 6-32: Bladder Wrack Seaweed (fucus vesiculosus).

Ulva (ulva lactuca) seaweed: Also known as "sea lettuce", is an edible green algae. They may be eaten raw, but are better boiled like other green vegetables, the water being strained off to lower the salt content.

Figure 6-33: Ulva (ulva lactuca) Seaweed.

	Calories	Grams Protein	Grams Fat	Grams Carbohydrate
1 lb Nettles	25.00	3.17	41.28	293
1 lb Dandelion	12.25	3.17	39.92	236
1 lb Sow Thistle	4.89	?	29.94	139
1 lb Cabbage	6.35	0.91	21.77	121

Figure 6-34: Value of Vegetable Food.

NOTE: The caloric value of the sow thistle is probably higher than the figure given because the fat, which has not yet been estimated, is omitted.

7

Firecraft

The ability to create and use fire was humankind's first significant step from the primitive, animal state to where we are now. Evidence for fire making dates to around 50,000 years ago; dozens of Neanderthal hand axes from France exhibit use-wear traces suggesting these tools were struck with the mineral pyrite to produce sparks. At the Neolithic site of La Draga, researchers have found that fungi was used as tinder. Hearths are one of the most common features found at archaeological sites. "Ötzi" – a.k.a. the Iceman - a well-preserved natural mummy of a man who lived between 3400 and 3100 BCE, found in September 1991 in the Ötztal Alps (hence the nickname "Ötzi"), carried material to make a fire (tinder fungus along with flint and pyrite for creating sparks).

In a survival situation, fire is a form of shelter, it provides warmth and can dry wet clothing. Fire can be used to boil and purify water, to prepare and preserve food. Fire is a very effective form of signaling. Fire can be used to harden wooden frog gigs and fish hunting spears. Last but not least, fire can boost morale – what Infantry and Special Forces refer to as "Ranger TV."

A. The Fire Triangle

Figure 7-1: The Fire Triangle.

Successful fire building requires three things to ignite and continue burning:

Heat: can be provided by lighters or matches (to include magnesium or ferrocerium rod and striker) or friction techniques, i.e. fire plow or fire drill.

Oxygen: can be supplied by blowing on the fire once flame has caught, but using a piece of cardboard or similar to fan flames is preferable. Tinder can be placed within kindling stacked into a platform to allow air (i.e. oxygen) to access your fire as it gets going.

Fuel: includes all the components of fire building, such as tinder, accelerants (such as petroleum or paraffin-soaked fuel) and kindling.

B. Fire Building Items

The key to successful fire building is in preparation. Set yourself up for success by gathering materials needed and have them standing by as you go about building your survival fire:

Figure 7-2: Tinder

Tinder: The smallest pieces of dry wood, bark or grasses, no wider than a pencil lead and no longer than your outstretched hand. In a conifer forest, dried pine needles make excellent tinder.

Figure 7-3: Kindling.

Kindling: pieces of wood no thicker than your thumb, about as long as your forearm.

Figure 7-4: Fuel.

Fuel: Pieces of wood about as thick as your wrist, as long as your arm; collect enough to last all night (a pile about 1-meter-long x 1 meter high (3' x 3').

A very effective tinder can be made by shaving down "Lighter Knot" wood tinder, or shavings from the inside of cedar or pine bark.

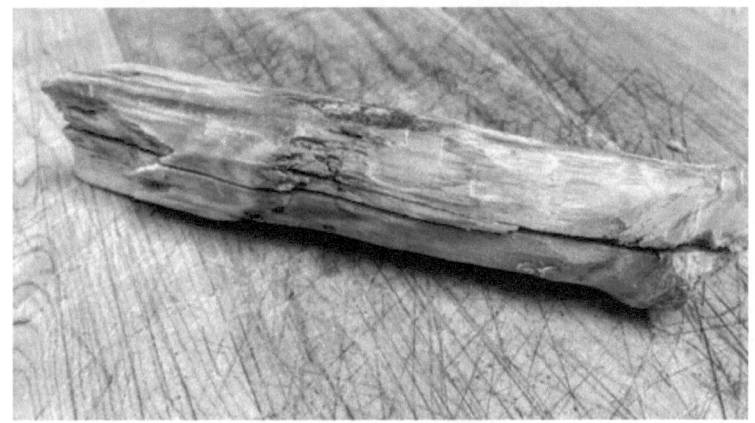

Figure 7-5: "Lighter Knot."

Figure 7-6: "Lighter Knot."

Figure 7-7: "Lighter Knot" shavings.

"Lighter knot", also known as "fatwood", "fat lighter", "lighter wood", "pine knot", or "heart pine", is derived from the heartwood of pine trees. After a tree has fallen, over time the resin-impregnated heartwood becomes hard and rot-resistant.

Although most resinous pines can produce fatwood, in the southeastern United States the wood is commonly associated with longleaf pine (pinus palustris).

Accelerants such as petroleum fuel-impregnated fibrous tinders are commercially available. These items are usually about the size of a cigarette filter; it is not necessary to use an entire piece, they can be shredded down and combined with natural tinder such as dead grass or wood shavings, so that many fires can be started with one piece of commercially available tinder.

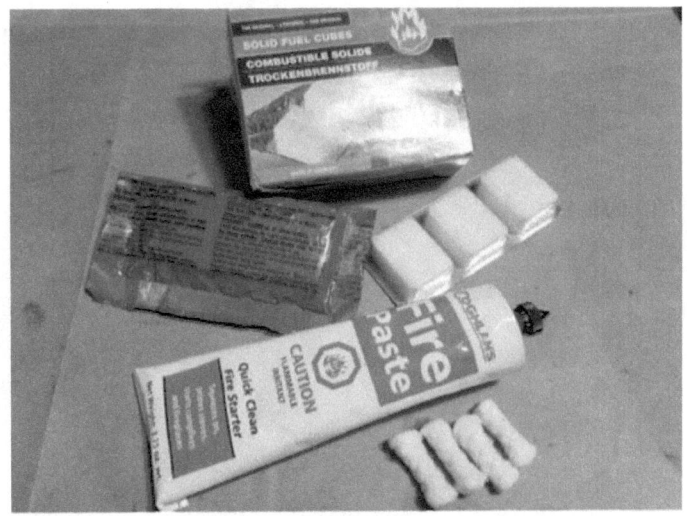

Figure 7-8: Commercially available fuels and accelerants.

Petroleum jelly (found in drugstores or the pharmaceutical part of your local supermarket) mixed with cotton balls produces a tinder similar to the commercially available tinders.

Bamboo is a useful in firecraft preparation. Use the shavings of dried bamboo as tinder. Split bamboo makes great kindling. Bamboo is also good material for fire plows and fire bows.

C. Primitive Fire-Starting Techniques

• Bow Drill friction fire method

• Fire Plow friction fire method

Both the bow drill and fire plow methods involve using friction to produce a spark, to cause tinder to smolder and then create a flame when blown upon. Both techniques require practice and a lot of patience. They are very labor intensive and take dedication to produce results.

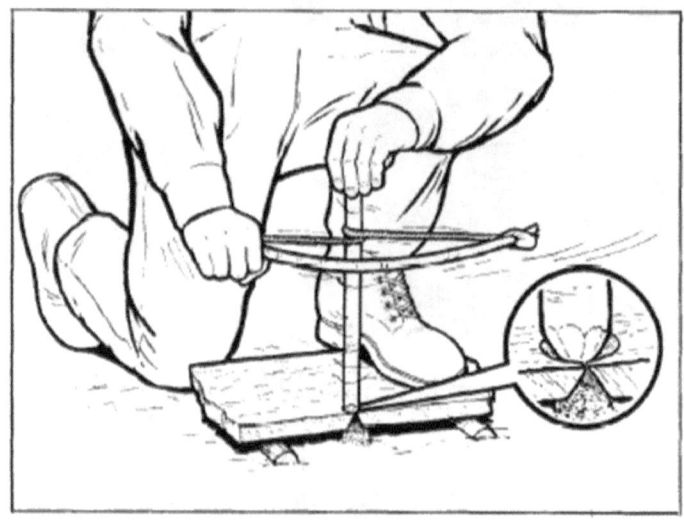

Figure 7-9: Bow drill method.

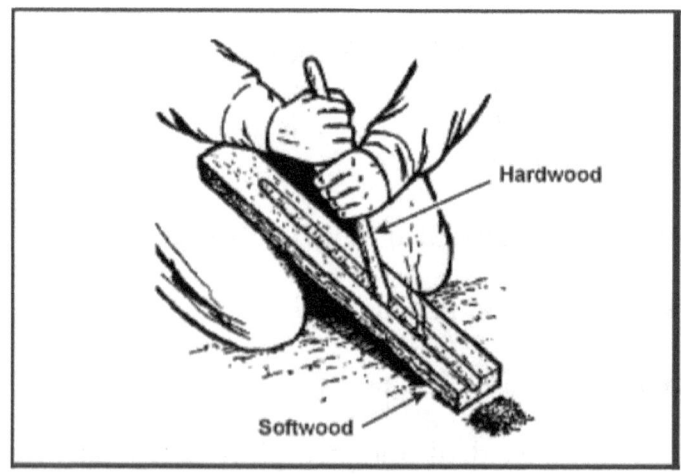

Figure 7-10: Fire Plow method.

D. Alternate Fire-Starting Techniques

Other methods for starting fires without matches or a lighter include ferrocerium rods and magnesium sticks, flint and steel, and the lens method.

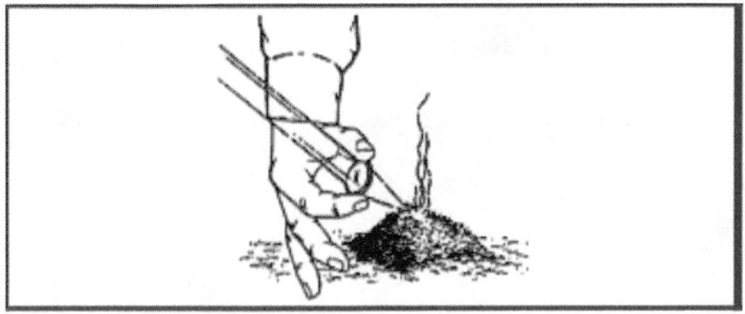

Figure 7-11: Lens method.

The lens method for starting fire only works on bright, sunny days. The lens can come from binoculars, a camera, telescopic sights, or magnifying glasses. A lens from a pair of spectacles can be used without removing it from the spectacles.

Angle the lens to concentrate the sun's rays on the tinder. Hold the lens over the same spot until the tinder begins to smolder. Gently blow or fan the tinder into a flame and apply it to the fire lay.

Ferrocerium rod (a.k.a. ferro rod) method of starting a fire includes a steel striker or scraper and of course some tinder. Ferrocerium rods are made from a mixture of cerium, lanthanum, iron and other metals. The striker or scraper is scraped along the ferro rod in strong, controlled strokes to produce sparks and ignite the tinder.

Figure 7-12: Ferro Rod Method.

A fixed-blade sheath knife can be used as a striker for a ferro rod but never scrape a ferro rod with the sharpened edge of your knife blade. Doing this will dull the knife blade. Instead, use the flat, squared-off back edge of the blade. If you don't have a knife, saw blade, or the striker that came with your ferro rod, broken glass works as an alternative striker. Hard rocks also make good scrapers.

A ferro rod by itself does not make a fire; ferro rods produce sparks. Tinder is required for the ferro rod method of making fire. The ferro rod is held close to very dry and fluffy tinder and scraped towards it so that the sparks can ignite the tinder.

A final word: while all the aforementioned techniques are effective, one cannot learn how to make fire from reading a book. Firecraft is a skill that needs to be practiced, and safe practices must be observed: clear your fire area of dry leaves and other flammable debris about six feet (2 meters) in all directions, keep in mind that sparks may travel from your fire to surrounding dry vegetation, steep the sides of your fireplace with dirt and rocks, and do not build your fire larger than what is required for survival purposes.

8

Signaling

Signaling includes two categories: electronic and visual (non-electronic). In bygone times, electronic signals systems were expensive and limited to military and large commercial operations, such as air transport or shipping. Nowadays, however, there are several options for private individuals to acquire a significant electronic signals capability, discussed below. Given the absence of electronics, visual signals techniques are also discussed.

A. Electronic Signaling

Nowadays, almost everyone in modern society is sends communications via electronic signaling, with modern cellular telephones. This then becomes your first priority means of communications in an emergency situation. Given the limitations of cellphones (proximity to towers, signal strength and battery life), the principle of redundancy requires us to have more than one method for electronic signaling.

Advantages of electronic signaling is instant communication and the ability to send and receive detailed information. Disadvantages of electronic signaling are that they require electrical power, which means there are limitations due to battery life, or power outages. Other disadvantages include range of signal, limitations due to terrain, or electronic interference.

Electronic communications alternatives include satellite phones, satellite messenger devices, Personal Locator Beacons (PLBs), Citizen Band (CB) radios, and Multi-Use Radio Service (MURS) radios.

Figure 8-1: Electronic signaling devices – Smartphone, Satellite Phone, Satellite Messenger/Personal Tracker, Personal Locator Beacon (PLB).

Cell Phone: In an emergency situation, use your personal cell phone SPARINGLY to conserve battery power. Store useful phone numbers such as police,

EMT/fire/rescue, and embassy (if traveling abroad) etc. Determine coverage in advance of travel excursions when possible. If you cannot get signal consider moving to higher ground, or away from overhead cover (such as dense foliage). Your phone may also include apps for mapping, navigation, tracking, GPS; learn how to use them – these are discussed in Section 11. Movement, under Land Navigation.

Satellite Phone: Unlike landline and cellular systems, satellite phones must have line-of-sight to a satellite to work. Satellite phone signals are obstructed by overhead cover such as in buildings or dense foliage. Satellite phones require a services subscription which is very expensive (prohibitively so to most people) but offer direct voice communications to any phone number on any phone network accessible to the general public.

Figure 8-2: Two Way Satellite Personal Trackers.

Two Way Satellite Personal Trackers: These devices are now commercially available that provide 2-way satellite messaging when beyond cellular range. As with satellite phones, an unobstructed view of sky is required for to acquire signal.

Capabilities include: send and receive non-emergency messages to cellphones or email addresses (some only send); works worldwide, (coverage varies by brand); tracking with map interface allows everyone to know you're OK; built-in compass and programmable waypoints; direct communication with Search & Rescue services in case of a life-threatening emergency; and rechargeable batteries. Annual Service plans are required but are quite affordable for frequent travelers and outdoors enthusiasts.

Personal Locator Beacon (PLB): PLBs are tracked by an international monitoring system, registered in the USA. The device is registered internationally to owner.

When you activate a PLB, a powerful distress signal is transmitted to a global system of satellites. The signal is routed via satellite to a network of response agencies, which ultimately results in your call for assistance reaching a Search and Rescue (SAR) agencies.

In the United States, those distress signals are monitored by the National Oceanic and Atmospheric Administration (NOAA). PLBs also acquire GPS-provided coordinates to pinpoint your location. A PLB with a strobe light can further aid rescuers when they search.

Responses won't be as robust in countries where search and rescue resources are limited, or course. PLBs must be registered (free of charge) in the NOAA SARSAT (Search and Rescue Satellite Aided Tracking) database. Your PLB unit's distress signal is then associated with vital personal information (name, address, emergency contact phone numbers and medical conditions, etc) that can assist your rescuers in their response. You must also update your data every two years and if you ever sell or transfer ownership of your PLB, you must report this in the database and the next user is then required to register their personal data.

PLBs are equipped with a long-lasting lithium battery, which remains dormant until you flip the switch to activate the PLB (a dormant PLB battery can last for five years)*.

Advantages of a PLB include:

• Works in remote areas worldwide**
• Able to transmit at -20°F (-28.9°C) for 24 hours; most PLBs will be able to transmit for than 30 hours in milder conditions
• Multi-year battery life (replacement requires sending it in)
• No subscription fees
• Stronger signal than a satellite messenger (unobstructed view of sky works best), however no ability to send messages or to cancel an SOS call.
Links to more information on PLBs are included in the References section at the back of this guide.
* Battery replacement requires the unit to be sent to a dealer and replacement costs are substantial.

** PLBs and satellite messengers don't all use the same satellite networks for SOS signals; all networks work fine in the U.S., but global reach varies. If you're going to a remote area, check the coverage map for the device(s) you are considering. Some countries don't permit the use of PLBs, so you need to contact foreign authorities if you plan to use your PLB abroad.

For all your electronics, have a means to recharge batteries, such as a generator, power adaptors and/or inverter for your vehicle, or a solar panel:

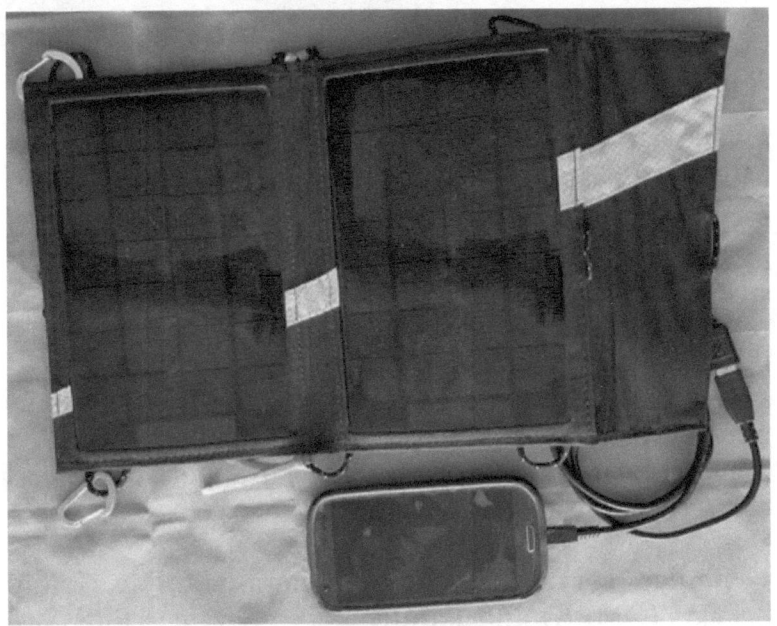

Figure 8-3: Solar Panel Battery Charger.

The Multi-Use Radio Service (MURS) is a two-way radio service similar to Citizens Band (CB) that does not require a license. The most common use of MURS channels is for short-distance, two-way communications using small, portable hand-held radios that function similar to walkie-talkies.

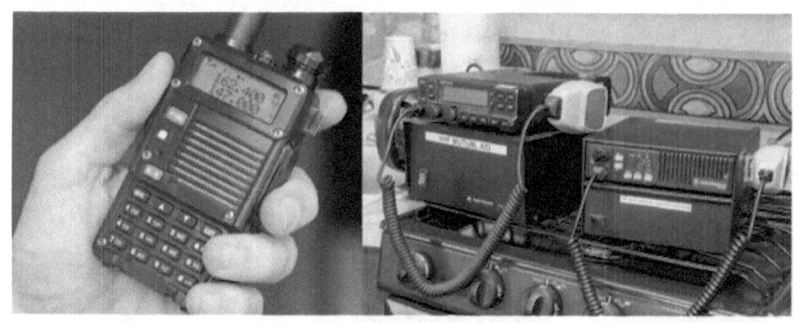

Figure 8-4: MURS Systems.

The FCC formally defines MURS as "a private, two-way, short-distance voice or data communications service for personal or business activities of the general public." MURS. uses a narrow selection of the VHF 151 – 154 MHz spectrum With a power limit of 2 watts, range operation is within 2-3 miles with a handheld unit, up to 10 miles with an externally mounted antenna. According to FCC regulation, MURS stations may not be connected to the public telephone network, may not be used for store and forward operations , and radio repeaters are not permitted.

Similar services include General Mobile Radio Service (GMRS) and Family Radio Service (FRS) are typically handheld portable devices that operate in UHF frequency band near 462 and 467 MHz. As such, signal is limited by obstructions; range is about 1 to 2 miles for handhelds, about 5 miles for vehicle mounted radios.

Figure 8-5: FRS/GMRS Systems.

Mobile and base station-style radios are available as well, but these are normally commercial UHF radios often used in the public service and commercial land mobile bands. GMRS licensees are allowed to establish repeaters to extend their communications range.

For effective communication, it is necessary to learn correct radio protocols, and the NATO phonetic alphabet.

If you are using MURS, FRS or MGRS systems within an organization, it will be necessary to develop a Signal Operating Instructions (SOI) including current and up-to-date information covering radio call signs and frequencies, a telephone directory, brevity codes and pro-words, and visual and sound signals. An SOI is compiled in a binder and distributed to communicators within the organization. Detailed information regarding developing this kind of capability, however, is beyond the scope of this guide.

Planning for signals capability involves the P.A.C.E. acronym: Primary / Alternate / Contingency / Emergency:

• Primary: Cell phone

• Alternate: MURS

• Contingency: FRS/GMRS

• Emergency: Satellite phone, Satellite Messenger, Personal Locator Beacons (PLB)

Contingency and Emergency signals can also be non-electronic/visual, such as ground-to-air signals (signal mirrors, panels, etc.), signal flares and signal fires (see below).

B. Visual (Non-Electronic) Signaling

I. Ground-To-Air Signals:

These may include prefabricated visual signal devices such as signal panels, signal mirrors and signal flares and smoke, such as used by the military. Signal panels can be made more effective by fastening them to sticks (as shown) creating a three-dimensional effect.

Improvised ground-to-air signals may include letters formed in the ground large enough to be seen from the air, enhanced by sticks, logs, palm fronds etcetera, or sheets or tarpaulins.

Figure 8-6: Ground-to-Air Signaling.

Figure 8-7: Improvised signal panels.

Figure 8-8: Signal fires.

NATO Phonetic Alphabet:

A	Alpha	AL FAH
B	Bravo	BRAH VOH
C	Charlie	CHAR LEE
D	Delta	DELL TAH
E	Echo	ECK OH
F	Foxtrot	FOKS TOROT
G	Golf	GOLF
H	Hotel	HOH TELL
I	India	IN DEE AH
J	Juliet	JEW LEE ETT
K	Kilo	KEY LOH
L	Lima	LEE MAH
M	Mike	MIKE
N	November	NO VEMBER
O	Oscar	OSS KAH

P	Papa	PAH PAH
Q	Quebec	KEW BEK
R	Romeo	ROW ME OH
S	Sierra	SEE AIR RAH
T	Tango	TANG OH
U	Uniform	YOU NEE FORM
V	Victor	VIK TAH
W	Whiskey	WISS KEY
X	X-ray	ECKS RAY
Y	Yankee	YANG KEY
Z	Zulu	ZOO LOO

II. Signal Flares & Fires:

These include commercially available flares such as flare guns, highway flares and signal smoke flares. Signal fires may include large bonfires, especially three in a row or in a triangle, or a single large fire (with leaves thrown on it to generate a column of smoke during the daytime).

Missing sailors rescued from Pacific island after SOS signal spotted in the sand – 08/04/2020.

Three men were rescued from a small, uninhabited Pacific island after writing a giant SOS sign in the sand. They were missing for three days in the Micronesia archipelago (near the Philippines) before their internationally recognized "S-O-S" distress signal (originated from Morse code) was spotted Sunday on the uninhabited Pikelot Island by searchers on Australian and U.S. aircraft.

Located in the western Pacific Ocean, the Federated States of Micronesia is comprised of more than 600 islands. The three-person crew aboard a 23-foot skiff set out from Pulawat atoll on Thursday. They intended to travel about 27 miles to Pulap atoll when they sailed off course and ran out of fuel.

The Australian Defense Force was asked for search and rescue support by the Rescue and Coordination Center in Guam on Saturday. The military ship, Canberra, which was returning to Australia from exercises in Hawaii, diverted to the area and joined forces with U.S. searchers from Guam.

The men were found in good condition about 118 miles from where they had set out. Their SOS message was first spotted by a U.S. Air Force plane, and an Australian Army helicopter was able to land on the beach to give the men food and water. A Micronesian patrol vessel picked them up.

Figure 8-9: Australia ARH-90 Helicopter lands on Pikelot Island (photo courtesy Australian Defense Force).

9

Medical Considerations

The circumstances leading to a survival or emergency situation may cause traumatic and/or environmental injuries. Comprehensive first aid and trauma medical training is beyond the scope of this guide; the objective of this section is - as much as possible – to impart a knowledge of survival self-aid and primitive medicine.

It is imperative that you learn basic first aid and trauma medicine – what to do for fractures, cuts, burns, etcetera. In a best case scenario, you'll have a well-stocked survival kit and a robust medical kit, but this guide does consider best case scenarios (quite the opposite, in fact). You must be prepared to survive and provide medical care with only the clothes on your back. You must know how to get along with what you have, to make do with little or nothing.

Immunization helps; keeping your vaccinations up to date prior to travel can save your life. Since January 2018, there have been 10 travel-related cases of yellow fever, including four deaths, reported among international travelers. None of the 10 travelers who succumbed to this deadly disease had received yellow fever vaccination.

A. Painkillers

Analgesics, or painkillers, are a must-have component of any field first-aid kit. A sprained ankle, jammed thumb, earache, or toothache can make any camping trip unpleasant, if not downright unbearable. Even minor injuries tend to throb painfully, especially at night, and they can rob you of the sleep you need to keep your body's immune system strong.

Ibuprofen, best known by its prescription-strength name Motrin, was made legal for over-the-counter sale a decade ago, and its value to an injured woodsman is hard to exaggerate. Each nonprescription-strength 200 milligram tablet delivers the same painkilling power as two acetaminophen (Tylenol) tablets, but unlike acetaminophen or aspirin, ibuprofen can be "stacked" to increase its potency. Up to four tablets can be safely ingested in a single dose (the equivalent of one 800-milligram Motrin dose) to quadruple the drug's analgesic strength. Ibuprofen's most common side effect is stomach irritation, which can be minimized by taking it on a full stomach and with plenty of water.

Aspirin also has a place in the first-aid kit, less as a painkiller than as an anti-coagulant. Doctors have long recommended that survivors of a heart attack ingest on aspirin a day to help keep their blood pumping more easily. More recently, it was discovered that chewing an aspirin at the onset of heart attack can lessen its severity and the damage it does to cardiac tissue.

NOTE: It's best to keep these medications in their original packaging, to avoid any suspicion of illegal drugs by law enforcement or customs officials.

(See Appendix A for a suggested inventory for a First Aid / Trauma Medical Kit)

B. Environmental Injuries

In any climate, seek shelter from the elements and drink plenty of water to prevent dehydration. If you are in a cold or wet climate, put on additional clothing to prevent hypothermia (in accordance with the COLDER principle of Looseness, and Layers). Hypothermia, dehydration, and other injuries related to the environment are included here because the primitive conditions of a survival or emergency situation increase to the likelihood of experiencing these types of injuries. In many cases, the treatment for these types of injuries is preventative in a nature.

I. Hypothermia

Exposure to cool or cold temperature over a short or long time can cause hypothermia; a condition that occurs when the body's core temperature drops below 95.0°F (35.0°C) as the body fails to maintain an inner core temperature of 97°F (36°C). When this happens a loss in body functions occur, including mental confusion and an increased risk of the heart stopping.

Dehydration and lack of food and rest predispose a person to hypothermia.

Hypothermia classically occurs from exposure to extreme cold, but as previously mentioned under Section 6. Shelter, hypothermia is not uncommon among hikers and other outdoors enthusiasts during warmer months.

The Centers for Disease Control and Prevention found that from 1999 to 2011 there were a total of 16,911 deaths in the United States caused by hypothermia.

The most common symptoms of hypothermia include:

• excessive shivering

• slowed breathing

• slowed speech

• clumsiness

• stumbling

• confusion

Someone who has excessive fatigue, a weak pulse, or who is unconscious may also be hypothermic. In treating a patient for shock, also treat for hypothermia. Immediate treatment is the key. Move the victim to the best shelter possible away from the wind, rain, and cold. Remove all wet clothes and get the victim into dry clothing.

Replace lost fluids with warm fluids, and warm the victim in a sleeping bag if possible, using direct contact via contact with another person's body. If the victim is unable to drink warm fluids, rectal rehydration may be used.

II. Dehydration

The signs and symptoms of dehydration vary depending on whether the condition is mild, moderate, or severe. Signs of mild to moderate dehydration include:

• Increased thirst (though not always)

• Dry mouth or skin

• Fatigue or mood swings

• Decreased urine output or darker urine

• Dizziness or fainting

Dehydration that progresses to a more severe state can bring about symptoms including:

• Dark amber or brown urine; decreased or no urine output

• Dizziness or lightheadedness affecting ability to walk

• Fever

• Muscle cramps

• Poor skin elasticity

• Lethargy or confusion

• Seizure

• Shock

Mild to moderate dehydration can be remedied by consuming fluids. Severe dehydration may require medical treatment, including intravenous fluid replacement.

III. Chilblains

Frostnip (or chilblains) begins as firm, cold and white or gray areas on the face, ears, and extremities that can blister or peel just like sunburn as late as 2 to 3 days after the injury. Chilblains are the result of tissue exposure to freezing temperatures and is the beginning of frostbite. The water in and around the cells freezes, rupturing cell walls, thus damaging the tissue.

Warming the affected area with hands or a warm object treats this injury. Wind chill plays a factor in this injury; preventative measures include layers of dry clothing and protection against wetness and wind.

IV. Trench Foot

Immersion or trench foot results from many hours or days of exposure to wet or damp conditions at a temperature just above freezing. The nerves and muscles sustain the main damage. In extreme cases the flesh dies and gangrene can occur, making it necessary to have the foot or leg amputated. The best prevention is to keep the feet dry. Carry extra socks in a waterproof packet. Dry wet socks inside clothing, against the body. Wash feet daily and put on dry socks.

V. Frostbite

This injury results from frozen tissues. Frostbite extends to a depth below the skin. The tissues become solid and immovable. Feet, hands, and exposed facial areas are particularly vulnerable to frostbite.

When with others, prevent frostbite by using the buddy system. Check your buddy's face often and make sure that he or she checks yours. If you are alone, periodically cover your nose and lower part of your face with your mittens.

Do not attempt to thaw the affected areas by placing them close to an open flame. Frostbitten tissue may be immersed in 99° to 109°F (37° to 42°C) water until thawed (water temperature can be determined with the inside wrist or baby formula method.) Dry the part and place it next to your skin to warm it at body temperature.

VI. Heat Injuries

There are three types of heat injuries: heat cramps, heat exhaustion and heat stroke. Signs, symptoms, and treatment for these injuries when medical help is not available are listed below.

Heat Cramps: The loss of electrolytes in the muscles due to excessive sweating causes heat cramps.

Symptoms are moderate to severe muscle cramps in legs, arms, or abdomen. These symptoms may start as a mild muscular discomfort. A person experiencing heat cramps should stop all activity, seek shade, and drink water. Fail to recognize the early symptoms and continued physical activity may lead to severe muscle cramps and pain. Treat as for heat exhaustion, below.

Heat Exhaustion: A large loss of body water and salt causes heat exhaustion. Symptoms are headache, mental confusion, irritability, excessive sweating, weakness, dizziness, cramps, and pale, moist, cold (clammy) skin. A person experiencing heat exhaustion must be immediately moved under shade, if possible, made to lie on a stretcher or similar item about 18 inches (45 centimeters) off the ground. Loosen his clothing. Sprinkle the victim with water and fan to cool the body and provide small amounts of water to drink every 3 minutes. Ensure the victim stays quiet and rests.

Heat Stroke: This is a medical emergency that if not treated immediately can result in permanent mental damage or death. The breakdown of the body's heat regulatory system - body temperature more than 105°F (40.5° C) - causes a heatstroke. Other heat injuries, such as cramps or dehydration, do not always precede a heatstroke. Signs and symptoms of heatstroke are:

• Swollen, beet-red face
• Reddened whites of eyes
• Victim not sweating

Unconsciousness or delirium, which can cause pallor, a bluish color to lips and nail beds (cyanosis), and cool skin.

NOTE: By this time, the victim is in severe shock. Cool the victim as rapidly as possible. Cool him by dipping him in a cool stream. If one is not available, douse the victim with water (urine, if necessary) or at the very least, apply cool wet compresses to all the joints, especially the neck, armpits, and crotch. Be sure to wet the victim's head (heat loss through the scalp is great) and fan the individual. Provide drinking fluids; treat for dehydration with lightly salted water and administer IVs (if available).

Expect the following symptoms during cooling:

• Vomiting

• Diarrhea

• Struggling

• Shivering

• Shouting

• Prolonged unconsciousness

• Rebound heatstroke within 48 hours

• Cardiac arrest; be ready to perform CPR

C. Snakebite and Envenomation

Chances of snakebite in a survival situation are minimal, if you take care to watch where you step, avoid thick underbrush, wear closed toe footwear and long pants.

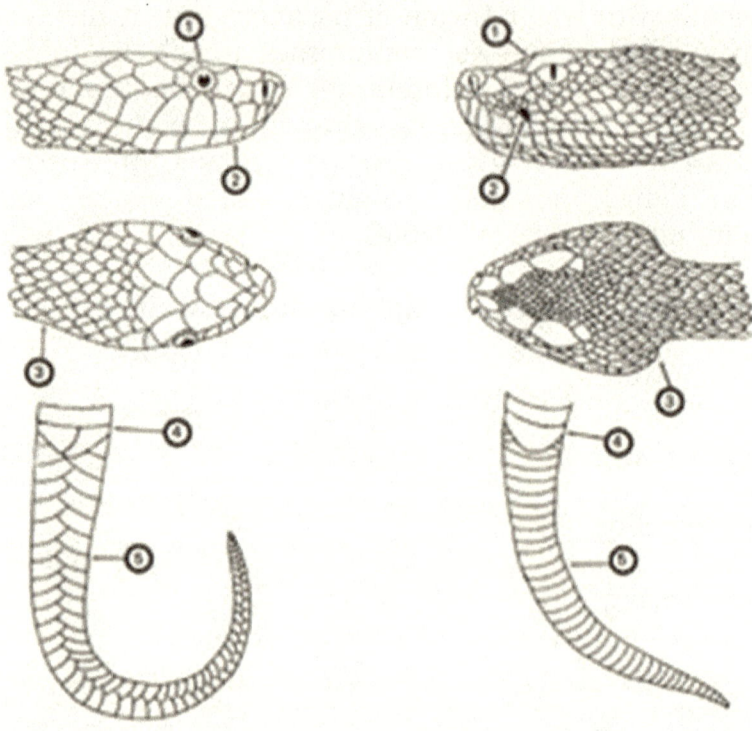

Figure 9-1: Nonvenomous vs. Venomous Snake (viper).

Clothing serves to increase the chances of a "dry" bite (no venom delivered). Snake bites are caused either from purposefully handling (upper extremities) or stepping on or near a snake (lower extremity).

There are two snake families that are of greatest concern; vipers (to include pit vipers) and elapids (cobras, coral snakes, mamba, and sea snakes). Elapids represent a huge variety of tropical and subtropical snakes and exist everywhere except Europe.

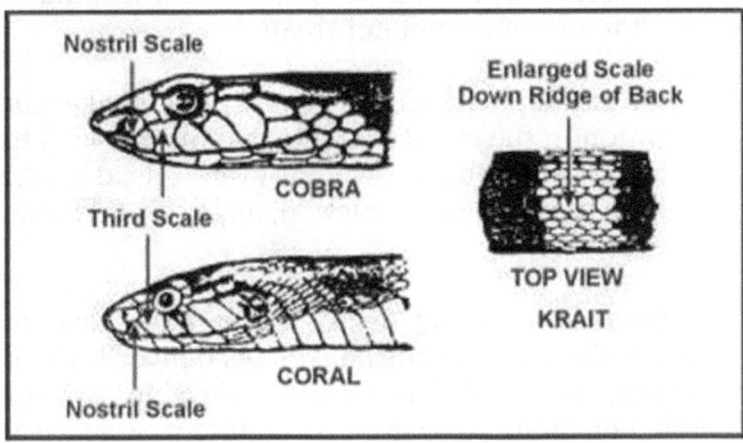

Figure 9-2: Elapids.

Look for these differences between non-venomous and venomous (viper) snakes:
• Pupil; nonvenomous round, venomous slit

• Heat sensitive "pit"

• Head; nonvenomous egg shaped, venomous triangular with narrow neck

• Subcaudal plates; nonvenomous double plates, venomous single plates

Generally, viper venom contains poisons that attack the victim's central nervous system (neurotoxins) while the venom of elapid's affect blood circulation (hemotoxins) although many snake's venoms contain elements of both types of poisons.

These poisons can cause a very large area of tissue death, leaving a large open wound, possibly leading to the need for amputation if not treated.

Do not attempt to capture or kill a snake for identification in the event of a bite, as this can lead to others being bitten; be aware that even a dead snake can still bite from reflexive reaction, up to several hours after death.

The good news is that deaths from snakebites are rare. More than 50% of the snakebites deliver little or no venom, and only about 25% develop serious systemic poisoning. However, snakebite in a survival situation can seriously affect morale, and failure to take preventive measures or failure to properly treat a snakebite can be catastrophic.

In treating a snakebite, determine whether the snake was poisonous or nonpoisonous; bites from a nonpoisonous snake will show rows of teeth. Bites from a poisonous snake will have distinctive puncture marks caused by fang penetration.

Symptoms of a poisonous bite may be spontaneous bleeding from the nose and anus, blood in the urine, pain at the site of the bite, and swelling at the site of the bite within a few minutes or up to 2 hours later. Breathing difficulty, paralysis, weakness, twitching, and numbness are also signs of neurotoxic venoms. These signs usually appear 1.5 to 2 hours after the bite.

If you determine that a poisonous snake bit an individual, take the following steps:

• Reassure the victim and keep him still.

• Set up for shock and force fluids or give by intravenous (IV) means.

• Remove watches, rings, bracelets, or other constricting items.

• Clean the bite area.

• Maintain an airway (especially if bitten near the face or neck) and be prepared to administer mouth-to-mouth resuscitation or CPR.

• Use a constricting band between the wound and the heart.

• Immobilize the site.

• Remove the poison as soon as possible by using a mechanical suction device. Do not squeeze the site of the bite.

US Army Field Manual 3-05.70 SURVIVAL includes the following guidance:

• Do NOT give the victim alcoholic beverages or tobacco products. Never give atropine! If available, give morphine or other central nervous system (CNS) depressors.

• Do NOT make any deep cuts at the bite site. Cutting opens capillaries that in turn open a direct route into the blood stream for venom and infection.

If medical treatment is over 1 hour away, make an incision (no longer than 6 millimeters [1/4 inch] and no deeper than 3 millimeters [1/8 inch]) over each puncture, cutting just deep enough to enlarge the fang opening, but only through the first or second layer of skin. Place a suction cup over the bite so that you have a good vacuum seal. Suction the bite site 3 to 4 times.

Suction for a MINIMUM of 30 MINUTES. Use mouth suction ONLY AS A LAST RESORT and only if you do not have open sores in your mouth. Spit the envenomed blood out and rinse your mouth with water. This method will draw out 25 to 30 percent of the venom.

• Do NOT put your hands on your face or rub your eyes, as venom may be on your hands. Venom may cause blindness.

• Do NOT break open the large blisters that form around the bite site.

After caring for the victim as described above, take the following actions to minimize local effects:

• If infection appears, keep the wound open and clean.

• Use heat after 24 to 48 hours to help prevent the spread of local infection. Heat also helps to draw out an infection.

• Keep the wound covered with a dry, sterile dressing.

• Have the victim drink large amounts of fluids until the infection is gone.

The primary concern in the treatment of snakebite is to limit the amount of eventual tissue destruction around the bite area. A bite wound, regardless of the type of animal that inflicted it, can become infected from bacteria in the animal's mouth. With nonvenomous as well as venomous snakebites, this local infection is responsible for a large part of the residual damage that results.

It is imperative to remain calm; shock and panic in a person bitten by a snake can also affect the person's recovery. Excitement, hysteria, and panic speeds up the circulation, causing the body to absorb the toxin quickly. Signs of shock occur within the first 30 minutes after the bite.

D. Invertebrate Bites and Stings

I. Insect Bites and Stings

Most insect bites and stings are mild; they might cause itching, swelling, and stinging that will go away in a day or two. Some bites or stings can transmit disease-causing bacteria, viruses, or parasites. Stings from bees, yellow jackets, wasps, hornets, and fire ants might cause a severe allergic reaction (anaphylaxis).

To treat a mild reaction to an insect bite or sting:

• Move to a safe area to avoid more bites or stings.

• Remove any stingers.

• Gently wash the area with soap and water.

• Apply a cloth dampened with cold water or filled with ice to the area of the bite or sting for 10 to 20 minutes. This helps reduce pain and swelling.

• If the injury is on an arm or leg, raise it.

• Apply to the affected area calamine lotion, baking soda paste, or 0.5% or 1% hydrocortisone cream. Do this several times a day until your symptoms go away.

• Take an anti-itch medicine (antihistamine) by mouth to reduce itching. Options include nonprescription cetirizine, fexofenadine (Allegra Allergy, Children's Allegra Allergy), loratadine (Claritin).

• The ointment sold under the tradename Tiger Balm effectively and instantly weakens itchy skin caused by mosquito bites, flies, and fire ants.

• Take a nonprescription pain reliever as needed.

Seek medical care if the swelling gets worse, the site shows signs of infection, or you don't feel well.

Anaphylaxis signs or symptoms:

A serious reaction may develop that suggests anaphylaxis:

• Trouble breathing

• Swelling of the lips, face, eyelids or throat

• Dizziness, fainting or unconsciousness

• A weak and rapid pulse

• Hives

• Nausea, vomiting or diarrhea

Even if it's just one or two signs or symptoms, if possible, call 911 or your local medical emergency number or seek other emergency care. Actions to take while waiting for medical help:

• If an epinephrine auto-injector (EpiPen, Auvi-Q, others) is available, inject the medication (usually done by pressing the auto-injector against the thigh and holding it in place for several seconds).

• Loosen tight clothing and cover the person with a blanket.

• Don't offer anything to drink.

• If needed, position the person to prevent choking on vomit.

Also known as adrenaline, epinephrine is a naturally occurring hormone that's used during the body's stress response. If epinephrine is administered via an auto-injector as an acute treatment to keep the patient's airway open, antihistamines (such as Benadryl) should also be taken to ensure the airway stays open after the epinephrine is out of the patient's system.

If epinephrine is not available, seek emergency treatment right away. In severe cases, untreated anaphylaxis can lead to death within half an hour.

Antihistamines are not sufficient to treat anaphylaxis. These medications can help relieve allergy symptoms but work too slowly in a severe anaphylaxis reaction.

NOTE: Epinephrine is the only first-line treatment for anaphylaxis; there is no substitute. Neither antihistamines nor glucocorticoids work as quickly as epinephrine, and neither can effectively treat severe symptoms of anaphylaxis.

Inserting a nasopharyngeal tube may hold an airway open in an emergency but may also cause injury to the airway. A last-ditch emergency measure may be to perform a cricothyrotomy. This is an advanced medical technique requiring skills that are beyond the scope of this book.

III. Spider Bite

Spider bites can be mistaken for other skin sores that are red, painful, or swollen. Be aware that skin sores attributed to spider bites may actually be bites from other bugs, such as ants, fleas, mites, mosquitoes and biting flies. Skin infections and other skin conditions, even burns, may also be mistaken for spider bites.

The process of determining if a sore is a spider bite might involve whether anyone saw a spider bite you, identifying the spider, and ruling out other possible causes of the signs and symptoms.

Almost all spiders, with only a few exceptions, produce venom, which serves the primary purpose of immobilizing their prey. Few spider species have large enough fangs to make them a threat to adult humans, but young children can be vulnerable to their bites.

Spider venoms are either necrotic (dissolving tissues surrounding the bite) or neurotoxic (impairing the nervous system). In some cases, the venom targets vital organs and systems.

Black Widow Identification:

Some clues for identifying black widow spiders include:

• Shiny black body with long legs

• Red hourglass shape on the belly

• Length of entire body, including legs, about 1 inch (2.5 cm) across

Brown Recluse Identification:

Some clues for identifying brown recluse spiders include:

• Golden or dark brown body with long legs

• Dark violin shape on top of the leg attachment segment

• Six eyes — a pair in front and a pair on both sides — rather than the usual spider pattern of eight eyes in two rows of four

• Central body is about 1/2 inch (1.2 cm) across

Treatment:

Most spider bites usually heal on their own in about a week. A bite from a recluse spider takes longer to heal and sometimes leaves a scar.

First-aid treatment for spider bites includes the following steps:

• Clean the wound with mild soap and water. Apply an antibiotic ointment three times a day to help prevent infection.

• Apply a cool compress over the bite for 15 minutes each hour. Use a clean cloth dampened with water or filled with ice. This helps reduce pain and swelling.

• If possible, elevate the affected area.

• Take an over-the-counter pain reliever as needed.

• If the affected area is itchy, an antihistamine, such as diphenhydramine (Benadryl) or certirizine (Zyrtec) might help.

• Observe the bite for signs of worsening or infection. You might need antibiotics if the bite develops into an open wound or becomes infected.

• For pain and muscle spasms, your doctor might prescribe pain medicine, muscle relaxants or both.

• A tetanus shot may be required.

Black Widow Antivenom:

If a black widow bite is causing severe pain or life-threatening symptoms, antivenom may be administered, usually given through a vein (intravenously). Symptoms usually ease within about 30 minutes of receiving the antivenom. As antivenom can cause serious allergic reactions, it must be used with caution.

III. Scorpion Sting

Most scorpion stings do not require medical treatment. Painkillers may be required if symptoms are severe. Scorpion antivenom may be given to prevent the development of symptoms.

Treatment:

• Clean the wound with mild soap and water.

• Apply a cool compress to the affected area. This may help reduce pain.

• Don't consume food or liquids if you're having difficulty swallowing.

• Take an over-the-counter pain reliever as needed. You might try ibuprofen (Motrin IB, Children's Motrin, others) to help ease discomfort.

• A tetanus shot may be required.

E. Primitive Medicine

Take the following information for what it is; the primitive medicine methods described below are the type of medicine practiced in prisoner-of-war camps and by primitive societies that live at near-Stone Age levels. Some of these techniques were practiced during ancient times by the Greeks, Romans, Arabs, Persians, and other cultures.

NOTE: The techniques described below are intended for the most extreme survival conditions when no other means are available and may or may not be effective. Results are not guaranteed.

I. Eat Everything

A basic principle of survival medicine is to eat. Whatever you find that is edible – dogs, cats, rats, snakes, weeds, bugs, or maggots - you must overcome revulsion and eat it. After the first time, strange ingredients really won't bother you. Rotten, maggot infested meat can be cooked maggots and all and eaten – maggots are protein, after all. Weeds can be boiled and eaten – as long as you're aware which poisonous plants to avoid – to remedy vitamin deficiencies. The point it you cannot afford to pass up a single bite when you are surviving at a subsistence level.

II. Foot Care

The importance of caring for your feet cannot be over-emphasized. Your feet are your primary means of transporting yourself out of whatever survival circumstances you might find yourself. The precautions are simple: if you have shoes or boots and socks, take them off periodically and rub your feet for five to ten minutes. If you have two pairs of socks, put on pair next to your skin to keep them dry. Change your socks at least once a day. When you bed down at night, take your shoes off. These proper precautions will prevent trench foot (immersion foot) and frostbite.

III. Dysentery

Dysentery is a problem is a common problem in survival situations. The risk of dysentery can be lessened if you properly purify your water (discussed above).

What is dysentery? An arbitrary standard is 25 stools per day. In a challenging environment, 8 to 10 can be considered normal, and 15 stools a day is simple diarrhea.

To treat dysentery, drink quantities of liquids, and eat, even if that means choking down food. Ingesting charcoal can help; scrape off charred portions of charred wood – about a handful – mix it with water into a slurry and swallow it. Any kind of bones can help; best if burned and ground into ash, but even dried bones can be ground between rocks into a powder. As with charcoal, mix with water and swallow the powder. Likewise, chalk (if available) can be ground into a powder and ingested to help cure dysentery.

Tree bark – any kind, but preferably from oak trees – boiled for 12 hours to three days (continue to add water as required) produces a black, vile tasting brew that contains tannic acid and will help to cure dysentery. It can also help further the healing of burns. Tea is also a cure for dysentery because it, too, contains tannin. Strong tea solutions which contain tannic acid in concentration, are a treatment for burns that has been used for centuries.

IV. Hepatitis

Hepatitis, or yellow jaundice, is a liver disease. Hepatitis causes loss of appetite; you don't want to eat but you must. In a survival situation, people suffering from hepatitis must be force fed despite their protesting otherwise.

V. Lice

These little insects (smaller than a grain of rice) can kill you. The average adult male has about 50,000 cc's of blood; a single louse sucks one cc of blood a day – a man covered in lice soon dies. Lice will bleed you to death unless you pick them off every single day. Keeping immunizations up to date will aid in preventing lice-borne diseases.

Lice breed at an exponential rate and must be picked off frequently. Regardless of how cold it is, inspect your entire body and every seam of clothing at least once a day and pick off every single louse. Lice hunting also helps fight off the mind-numbing boredom that can accompany a survival situation.

VI. Intestinal Worms

All kinds of worms – hook, round, and tape worms - will infest you from the food you eat and from the dirt and filth where you live. Symptoms include live worms crawling out of one's throat or nose. Personal hygiene is the best preventive measure against parasitic infestations. Wash your body and clothes often, as well as you can. A remedy for worms is to drink one or two tablespoons of kerosene or gasoline. Kerosene is more effective, but gasoline will do; both will make you feel sick, but it will kill off the worms.

VII. Pneumonia

As your immune system weakens and resistance to disease lowers, pneumonia is a common malady, especially in winter and it can make one extremely sick. According to prisoner of war anecdotes, without antibiotics, there is only one remedy: keep a sick individual on his or her feet. Not twenty-four hours a day, but do not let a person with pneumonia lie down, pull something over their head and roll over to face the wall; a person who does this will die. The sick individual must be kept alert and interested, or he or she will not survive.

VIII. Bleeding

Contrary to trauma medicine practice, in a long-term survival situation DO NOT apply a tourniquet.

A tourniquet destroys tissue, gangrene sets in, which can be lethal. Instead, apply constant heavy pressure – this will stop 99% of all bleeding. In the case of arterial bleeding, attempt to stop the blood from spurting out by sticking a finger into the wound and hold it there.

IX. Burns

Wash out the burned area and cover it with a sterile dressing. If there is no sterile water available, you can use urine; it is 100% sterile, coming out of the body. Under extreme circumstances it will not hurt you and it may save your life. As stated earlier, tannic acid is good for burns; there is tannic acid in strong boiled bark and tea solutions.

X. The Water Cure

Hot water can treat everything from headaches to athlete's foot.

If you have nothing else, soaking an injury or wound in hot water may not help in every case but it will keep the patient busy doing something that seems reasonable and purposeful. Sitting for two or three hours soaking a body part takes one's mind off unfortunate circumstances and promotes positive thoughts about a cure that may be in effect and may actually make the patient feel better.

For stomach aches, a possible variation is to heat a brick or stone, wrap it in cloth and put it over your stomach.

XI. Wounds and Surgery

There are three treatments for a wound under extreme conditions:

• Wash it out with hot water (if possible)

• wash it out with urine, and

• pick out all foreign matter.

Good medicine says never to stick our fingers in a wound, but if you have nothing else and if there are pieces of metal or bits of clothing in the wound, pick or dig them out with your fingers.

Before the development of antibiotics (immediately prior to World War II) maggot therapy was an accepted treatment for infected wounds. Maggots only eat dead tissue and will clean out a wound better than anything else except maybe surgery. To acquire maggots, just expose the wound – flies will come, and maggots will follow.

If surgery of any kind is required, remember that the area of a wound is dead. When you realize there is no feeling in a wound, it is easier for you to stick a needle into it, to cut, or to do whatever else is necessary.

For boils, cysts, and the like, soak the area in hot water for a couple of days and then if it is still necessary, lance it with a sharp knife.

XII. Summary

Medical considerations covered within this chapter provide informational guidance only and do not replicate formal training in first aid and trauma medicine. Seek this training from emergency responder resources, community college courses and organizations such as the Red Cross, etc.

In a survival or other emergency situation, a basic first aid kit and/or a trauma medical kit are absolute luxury items; you must be prepared for the possibility or even probability that emergency treatment may extend far beyond what was covered in your training. You may be the only person available to provide treatment, with only improvised medical supplies such as belts, rags, and field knives.

Many things are possible to those with will and determination. Under extreme circumstances, people with severe wounds have stuffed them with handkerchiefs, bound them with torn shirts, amputated a limb even, whittled a crutch and kept going. Under extreme circumstances you are only limited by your imagination, faith, and optimism.

10

Movement

In a survival situation, you may be fortunate to have a GPS or a map and compass, and you may be able to move toward help and recovery. Navigation using a map and compass is a necessary survival skill. In addition, you must also learn how to navigate using the sun and the stars.

A. Map Reading and Land Navigation

The ability to know where you are, to find your location on a map, to navigate to a known point, and to communicate your location in map reference coordinates are essential survival skills. The US Army's Field Manual 3-25-26 MAP READING & LAND NAVIGATION requires about forty hours of classroom and practical application to train soldiers on its contents, cover-to-cover. This is beyond the scope of this survival guide, however there are some useful navigation skills that are reviewed here:

• Read and plot coordinates from a map and/or a GPS

• Use a map and compass together

• Navigate to selected points using compass, GPS and/or cell phone compass

Given proper resources, these skills may be acquired in a relatively short period of time. However, learning these skills requires hands-on, performance-based training in the field; this book does not replicate that. But the basics can be learned with a discussion of what a map actually is, what information can be derived from it, and how a map and compass assist in moving from one place to another.

I. Read and plot coordinates from a map and/or a GPS

A map is a graphic representation of the earth's surface drawn to true north and to scale, as seen from above, and reproduced in two dimensions. Coordinate systems overlaid upon a map allow one to accurately determine one's position.

Latitude / Longitude Coordinate system:

One of the oldest methods of determining location on a map is based upon the geographic coordinate system. It is important to understand the basics of this system, because you may be required to report your location in geographic coordinates (or simply 'geo coordinates'), expressed in degrees, minutes and seconds.

The geographic coordinate system is an imaginary set of east-west rings around the globe (parallel to the equator), and a set of north-south rings crossing the equator at right angles and converging at the poles (meridians). These parallels and meridians form a network of reference lines from which any point on the earth's surface can be located.

The distance of a point north or south of the equator is known as its latitude. The rings around the earth parallel to the equator are called parallels of latitude or simply parallels. Lines of latitude run east-west but north-south distances are measured between them.

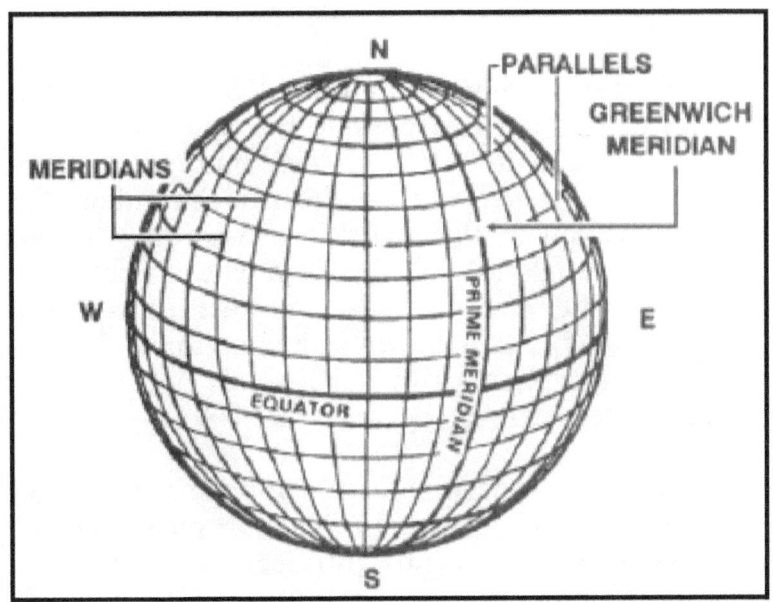

Figure 10-1: Reference Lines.

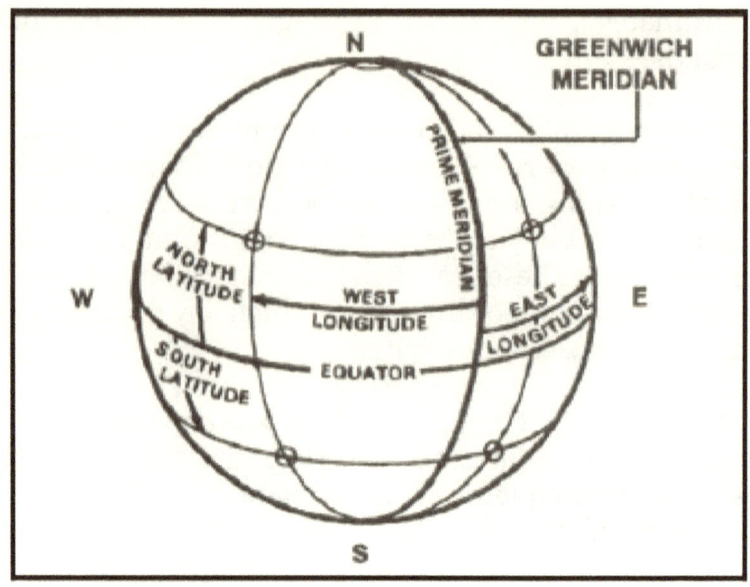

Figure 10-2: Prime Meridian and Equator.

A second set of rings around the globe at right angles to lines of latitude and passing through the poles is known as meridians of longitude or simply meridians. One meridian is designated as the prime meridian. The prime meridian of the system we use runs through Greenwich, England and is known as the Greenwich meridian. The distance east or west of a prime meridian to a point is known as its longitude. Lines of longitude (meridians) run north-south but east-west distances are measured between them.

Geographic coordinates (or simply "geo coordinates") are expressed in angular measurement. Each circle is divided into 360 degrees, each degree into 60 minutes, and each minute into 60 seconds. Degrees are symbolized by °, minute by ', and second by ". Starting with 0° at the equator, the parallels of latitude are numbered to 90° both north and south. The extremities are the North Pole at 90° north latitude and the South Pole at 90° south latitude. Latitude can have the same numerical value north or south of the equator, so the direction N or S must always be given.

Starting with 0° at the prime meridian, longitude is measured both east and west around the world. Lines east of the prime meridian are numbered to 180° and identified as east longitude; lines west of the prime meridian are numbered to 180° and identified as west longitude. The direction E or W must always be given. The line directly opposite the prime meridian, 180°, may be referred to as either east or west longitude.

Geo coordinates appear on all standard maps; on some, they may be the only method of locating and referencing a specific point. The four lines that enclose the body of the map (neat lines) are latitude and longitude lines. Their values are given in degrees and minutes at each of the four corners.

In addition to the latitude and longitude given for the four corners, there are, at regularly spaced intervals along the sides of the map, small tick marks extending into the body of the map. Each of these tick marks is identified by its latitude or longitude value.

To illustrate the proper way to write geographic coordinates, assume that a person needs to write the coordinates of where they're located, 30°20' north of the equator and 135°6' east of the prime meridian. Thus, the position is located at 30°20' north latitude and 135°06' east longitude. By combining latitude and longitude, the position of the geographic location can be expressed as 30°20'N/135°06'E (stated "thirty degrees, twenty minutes north, one hundred thirty-five degrees, six minutes east").

In reporting your position using geo coordinates, be aware that there are actually three formats of latitude and longitude, each in widespread use, and each having punctuation sub-variants:

• Degrees-Minutes-Seconds (DMS): N 38°53'23.3", W 077°02'11.6"

• Degrees-Minutes-Decimal minutes (DMM or DDM): 38°53.388' N, 077°02.193' W

• Decimal Degrees (DDD or DD): 38.88980°, -077.03654°

In general, when writing geographic coordinates:

• Write latitude first, followed by longitude.

• Use an even number of digits for latitude and an odd number of digits for longitude.

• Do not use a dash or leave a space between latitude and longitude.

• Use single upper-case letter to indicate direction from the equator and prime meridian.

• Include the symbols for degrees, minutes, and seconds.

Universal Transverse Mercator (UTM) Grid

The geo coordinate system is important to understand the fundamentals of geography, and is useful for ships at sea or aircraft, moving over vast distances. However, for the shorter distances and areas associated with ground movement, grid reference systems have been developed. These systems are based on a series of maps that represent portions of the world as flat two-dimensional squares (think of a globe covered in postage stamps; each postage stamp would be a zone of the grid system, or a 'grid zone').

The Universal Transverse Mercator (UTM) grid system was adopted by the U.S. Army in 1947 and is currently used by U.S. and NATO armed forces. With the advent of inexpensive GPS receivers, many other map users are adopting the UTM grid system for coordinates that are simpler to use than latitude and longitude.

The UTM grid system is based on a flat world, not a sphere. On maps based on UTM, the grid lines and the lines of latitude and longitude don't match up.

The US National Grid (USNG) and the Military Grid Reference System (MGRS) are geographic coordinate systems that come from the UTM grid system. They are, for all practical purposes, identical; the difference being the USNG includes spaces between grid zones and grid values when expressing coordinates, whereas the MGRS dos does not include spaces. The USNG was adopted as a national standard by the Federal Geographic Data Committee (FGDC) of the US Government in 2001.

UTM has in many coordinate systems. Map Datum sets the coordinate system on which the map is structured. Map Spheroid shows the coordinate system the device is using. The coordinate system for USNG / MGRS is WGS 84.

How the USNG / MGRS works

The USNG is an alpha-numeric reference system that overlays the UTM coordinate system. Briefly, an example of a full USNG spatial address (grid reference) is:

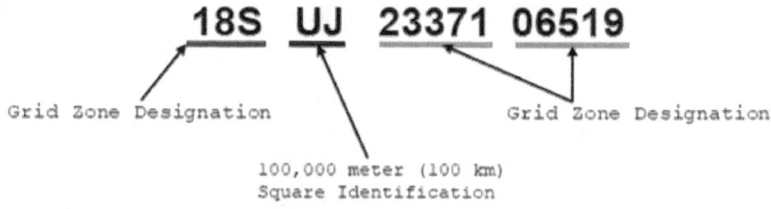

Figure 10-3. MGRS. (This example is the grid reference of the Jefferson Pier in Washington DC, within 1 meter).

Grid Zone Designation (GZD): this indicates a world-wide unique address. This consists of up to 2 digits (6-degree longitude UTM zone) for West to East, followed by a letter (8-degree latitude band) from South to North; in this example, "18S". 100,000 meter (100 km)

Square Identification: this narrows the Grid Zone down to regional areas. This consists of two letters, the first West to East, the second South to North; in this example, "UJ".

Grid Coordinates: these are coordinates for specific locations within local areas. This part consists of an even number of digits, in this example, 23371 06519, and specifies a location within the 100 km grid square, relative to its lower-left corner.

Split in half, the first part (here 23371), called the "easting", gives the displacement east of the left edge of the square; the second part (here 06519), called the "northing", gives a distance north of the bottom edge of the containing square.

Depending on the required precision, a grid reference is usually expressed to less than the full 10 digits. These values represent a point position for an area's southwest corner:

• Ten digits (23371 06519) locate a point within a 1-meter square.

• Eight digits (2337 0651) locate a point within a 10-meter square.

• Six digits (233 065) locate a point within a 100-meter square.

• Four digits (23 06) locate a point within a 1,000-meter (1 kilometer) square.

• Two digits (2 0) locate a point within a 10,000-meter (10 kilometer) square.

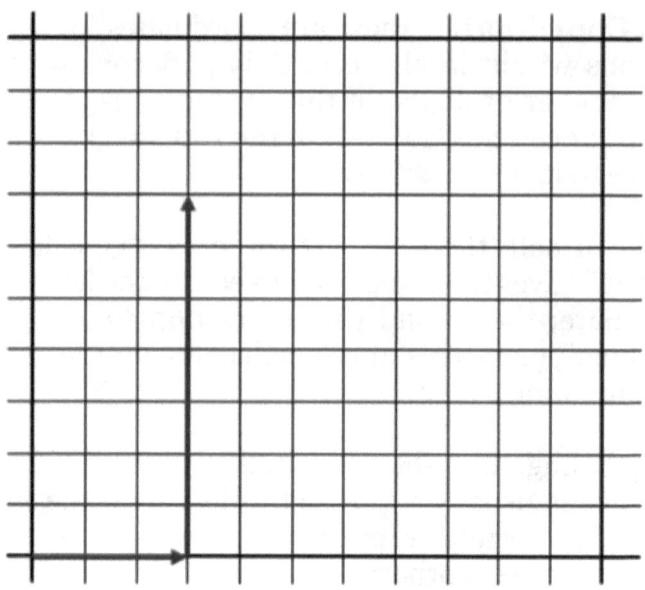

Figure 10-4: "Right, and then Up."

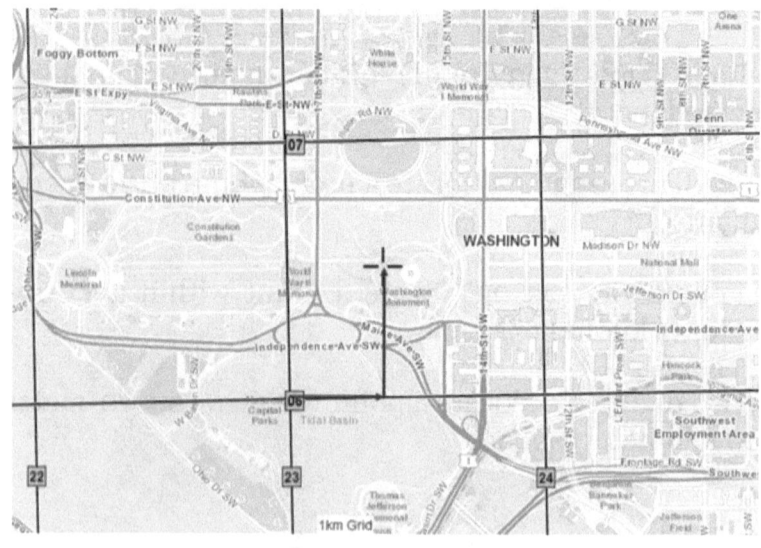

Figure 10-5: "Right, and then Up."

(The above example is 18S UJ 23371 06519, the grid reference of the Jefferson Pier marker in Washington DC, within 1 meter).

Coordinates are always read "Right, and then Up" (as XY Cartesian coordinates) with the X first and Y second. This contrasts with Lat/Long geo coordinates, which generally have latitude (Y) first. Determine what your destination is by associating it with actual features on the map (i.e., intersection of East-West running road and a North-South running stream).

A coordinate scale can be fabricated or purchased commercially, to assist with determining location on a map using UTM grid coordinates.

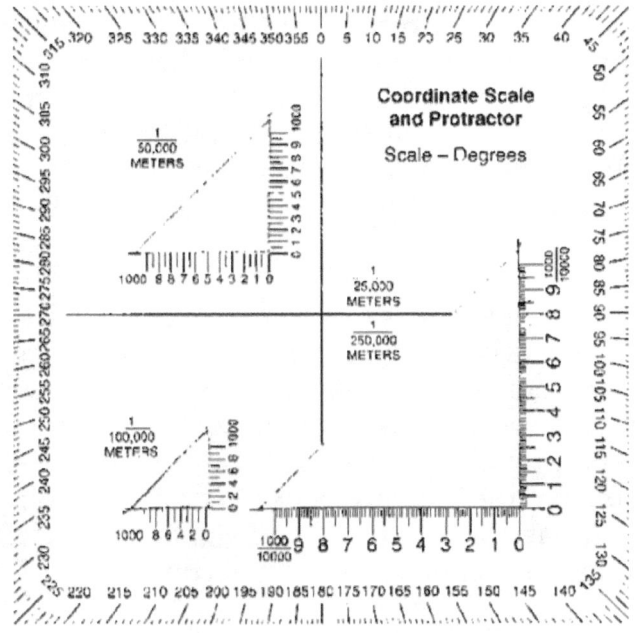

Figure 10-6: Coordinate Scale & Protractor.

Relay Coordinates to Recovery Personnel

Given a GPS, or the ability to determine your location on a map, and the opportunity to communicate electronically (cell phone, radio or satellite phone) you must be able to state your coordinates so that rescue assets can move to recover you. As mentioned above, these coordinates will be expressed in geo coordinates (latitude and longitude) or UTM grid coordinates.

A growing number of software applications incorporate or refer to the US National Grid. Links for some of these, including The National Map (USGS) are listed in References.

These applications include conventional mapping applications with overlaid USNG grid and/or coordinate readouts, and several "you-are-here" mobile applications which give the user's current USNG coordinates, such as USNGapp.org and FindMeSAR.com; mobile applications that give the user's current coordinates, e.g., for relay on calls for help.

The purpose of a map is to permit one to visualize an area of the earth's surface with pertinent features properly positioned. Maps in use today by engineers, geologists, surveyors, the military, and outdoors enthusiasts provide information on the existence, location of, and the distance between ground features, indicate variations in terrain, heights of natural features, and the extent of vegetation cover.

Topographic maps portray terrain features in a measurable way, as well as the horizontal positions of the features represented. The vertical positions, or relief, are normally represented by contour lines. On maps showing relief, the elevations and contours are measured from a specific vertical datum plane, usually mean sea level.

Topographic maps are commonly found in large almanacs in stores that cater to outdoorsmen and hunters.

There is a free online resource; GISsurfer Interactive Maps[4] that provides topographical maps of most of the Earth's surface, in various formats and grid references.

It is my habit to consult this resource before setting off on a journey. Screenshots can be made of the area you expect to be in and printed out for an actual paper copy of the map, suitable for plotting locations and determining azimuths (direction of travel).

Place your map in zip lock plastic bag to protect it from wear and tear and to keep it waterproof.

Marginal information:

Along the edges of a standard map are the marginal information and symbols, where useful information about the map is located and explained.

---

[4] https://mappingsupport.com/p2/gissurfer-interactive-recreation-disaster-maps.html

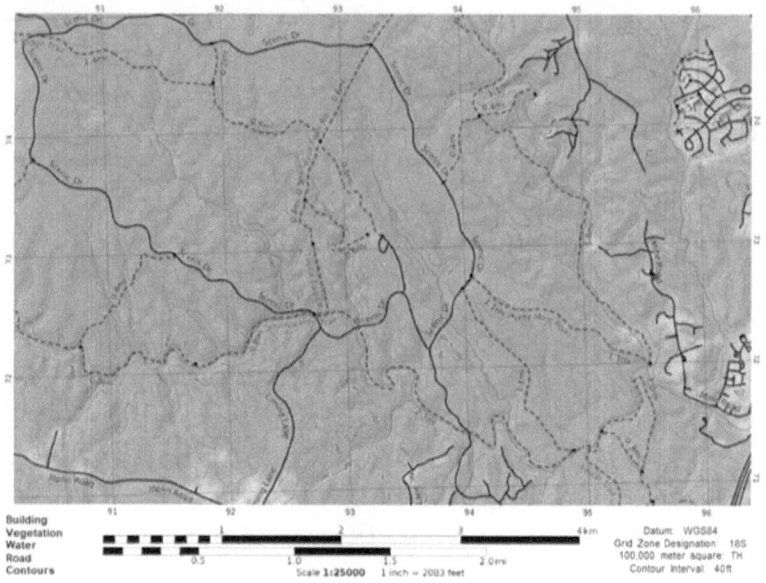

Figure 10-7: Marginal Information.

Not all maps are the same, so it becomes necessary every time a different map is used to examine the marginal information carefully. Information includes such items as:

Sheet Name: A map is generally named for the settlement contained within the area covered by the sheet or for the largest natural or manmade feature located within the area at the time the map was drawn. Scale: Because a map is a portion of the earth's surface drawn to scale, it is important to know what scale is used.

This allows you to determine ground distances between objects or locations on the map, the size of the area covered, and the amount of detail depicted. The scale of a map is the ratio between the distance on a map and the corresponding distance on the surface of the earth. Scale is expressed as a representative fraction; map distance is the numerator and ground distance is the denominator - the larger the number after 1: the smaller the scale of the map.

• **Small**: a standard small-scale map is 1:1,000,000 (1 inch of map=1,000,000 inches of ground). This map covers a very large area at the expense of detail.

• **Medium**: a medium-scale map is 1:250,000. Contain a moderate amount of detail. (1inch on map = 250,000 inches ground distance).

• **Large**: maps with scales of 1:75,000 and larger cover small areas, but with much greater detail. The standard large-scale map is 1:50,000.

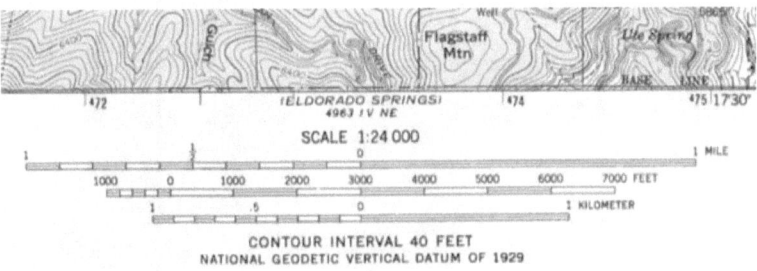

Figure 10-8: Sample Map Marginal Data, Bar Scale & Contour Interval.

Bar Scale: Located in the center of the lower margin are rulers used to convert map distance to ground distance. Maps have three or more bar scales, each in a different unit of measure.

Contour Interval Note: states the vertical distance between adjacent contour lines of the map. When supplementary contours are used, the interval is indicated.

Elevation Guide: Normally found in the lower right margin. It is a miniature characterization of the terrain shown. The terrain is represented by bands of elevation, spot elevations, and major drainage features. The elevation guide provides the map-reader with a means of rapid recognition of major landforms.

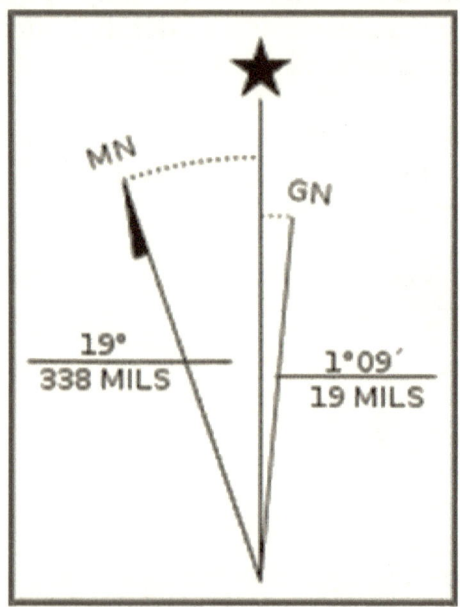

Figure 10-9: Declination Diagram.

Declination Diagram: This is used to indicate the angular relationship between true, grid, and magnetic north and is represented by prongs.

While the relative position of the prongs are correct, they are seldom plotted to scale. Do not use the diagram to measure a numerical value. This value will be written in the map margin beside the diagram.

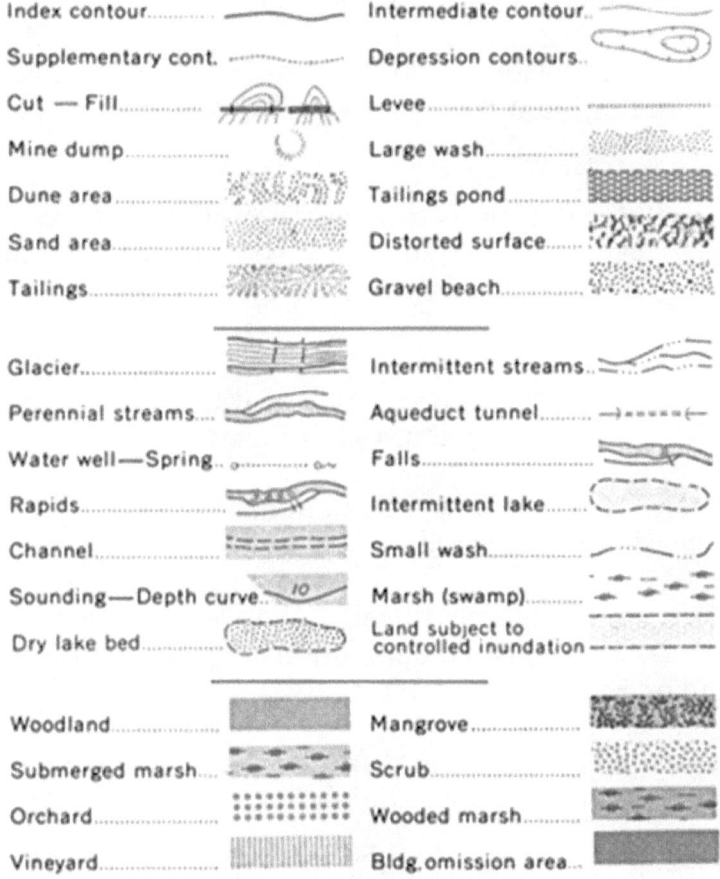

Figure 10-10: Sample Map Legend.

Legend: Located in the lower left margin, a map's legend illustrates and identifies the topographic symbols used to depict some of the more prominent features on the map. The symbols are not always the same on every map. Always refer to the legend to avoid errors when reading a map.

Use of Colors on Maps: Generally, features are depicted by the following colors:

• **Black**: indicates cultural (man-made) features such as buildings and roads, surveyed spot elevations, and all labels.

• **Red Brown**: used to identify cultural features, all relief features, non-surveyed spot elevations, and elevation, such as contour lines on red-light readable maps.

• **Blue**: identifies hydrography or water features such as lakes, swamps, rivers, and drainage.

• **Green**: identifies vegetation, such as woods, orchards, and vineyards.

• **Brown**: identifies all relief features and elevation, such as contours on older edition maps, and cultivated land on red-light readable maps.

• **Red**: classifies cultural features, such as populated areas, main roads, and boundaries, on older maps.

• **Other**: occasionally other colors may be used to show special information. These are indicated in the marginal information as a rule.

Contour Lines: These lines show relief and elevation on a standard topographic map. A contour line represents an imaginary line on the ground, above or below sea level. All points on the contour line are at the same elevation. The elevation represented by contour lines is the vertical distance above or below sea level.

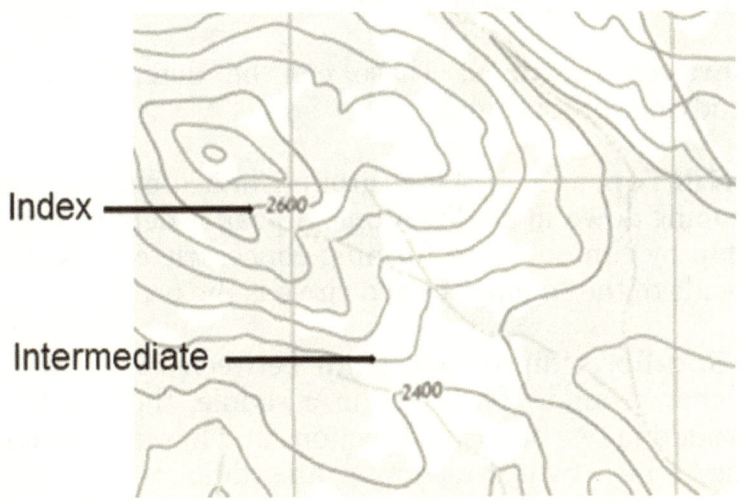

Figure 10-11: Contour Lines, Index & Intermediate.

The three types of contour lines used on a standard topographic map are as follows:

• **Index**: starting at zero elevation or mean sea level, every fifth contour line is a heavier line. These are known as index contour lines. Normally, each index contour line is numbered at some point. This number is the elevation of that line.

• **Intermediate**: contour lines falling between the index contour lines are called intermediate contour lines. These lines are finer and do not have their elevations given. There are normally four intermediate contour lines between index contour lines.

• **Supplementary**: these contour lines resemble dashes. They show changes in elevation of at least one-half the contour interval. These lines are normally found where there is very little change in elevation, such as on fairly level terrain.

Terrain features: These can be determined by studying contour lines.

• **Hill Top**: an area of high ground, indicated by terrain sloping down in all directions. A peak is depicted on a map by contour lines forming concentric circles. The inside of the smallest closed circle is the peak.

• **Saddle**: a dip or low point between two areas of higher ground. If you are in a saddle, there is high ground in two opposite directions and lower ground in the other two directions. A saddle is normally represented by contour lines forming an hourglass.

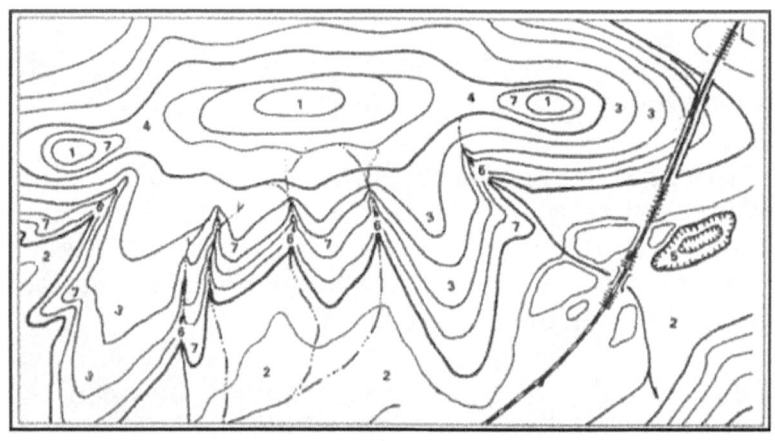

Figure 10-12: Terrain Features; 1. Hilltop, 2. Valley, 3. Ridge, 4. Saddle, 5. Depression, 6. Draw, 7. Spur.

• **Ridge**: a sloping line of high ground. Contour lines forming a ridge tend to be U-shaped or V-shaped. The closed end of the contour line points away from high ground.

• **Drainage**: contour lines forming an area of drainage are either U-shaped or V-shaped. To determine the direction water is flowing, look at the contour lines. The closed end of the contour line (U or V) always points upstream or toward high ground.

• **Depression**: a low point in the ground or a sinkhole; an area of low ground surrounded by higher ground in all directions, or simply a hole in the ground. Usually only depressions that are equal to or greater than the contour interval will be shown. On maps, depressions are represented by closed contour lines that have tick marks pointing toward low ground.

• **Type of Slope**: Where the lines become closer, the slope is steeper; the farther apart the lines, the gentler the slope.

The National Map:

Part of the U.S. Geological Survey (USGS) National Geospatial Program, the National Map is the official replacement for the USGS topographic map program. The geographic information available includes orthoimagery (aerial photographs), elevation, geographic names, hydrography, boundaries, transportation, structures and land cover. The National Map is accessible via the Web, as products and services, and as downloadable data.

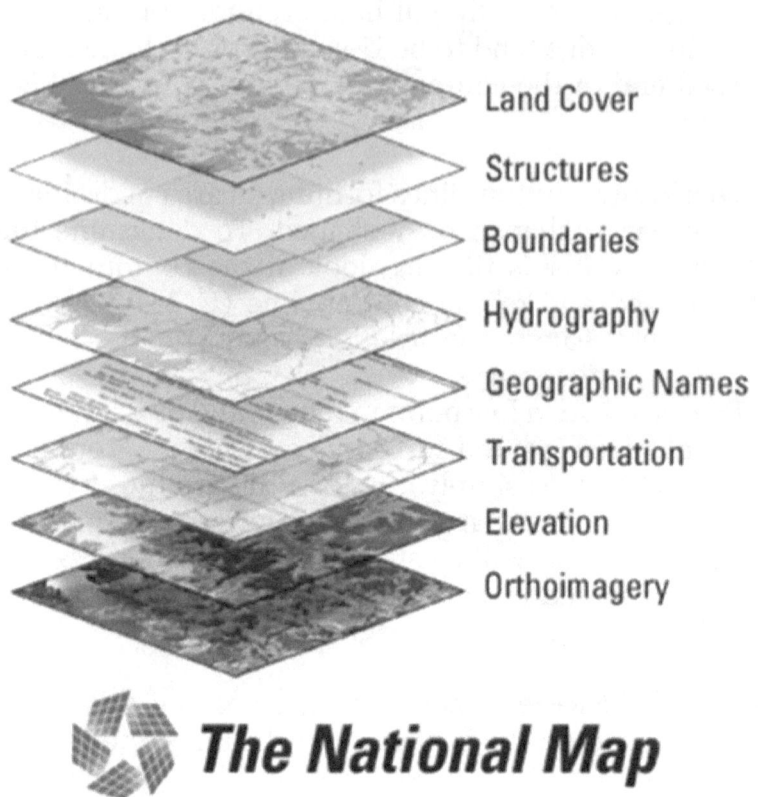

Figure 10-13: The National Map.

The National Map is the official replacement for the USGS topographic map program; its uses range from recreation to scientific analysis to emergency response. Mission Manager, the most widely used incident management software tool for first responders, integrates the USNG in its functionality.

USNGapp.org :

Figure 10-14: USNGapp.org.

USNGapp.org is a free browser-based app which shows a mobile user's current USNG location. Once loaded, the app works without an Internet connection.

II. Use a Map and a Compass Together

A compass is an instrument used for navigation and orientation that shows direction relative to the geographic cardinal directions. Many modern floating needle compasses incorporate a baseplate that includes a coordinate scale tool. These types of compasses may be referred to as "orienteering", "baseplate" or "map compass" designs.

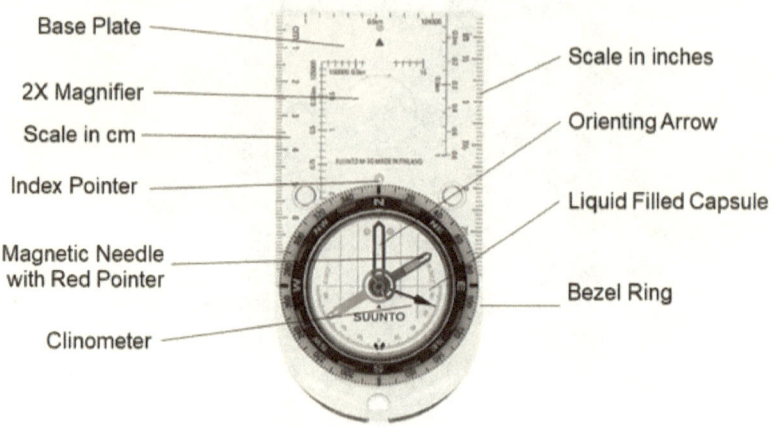

Base Plate

Scale in inches

2X Magnifier

Orienting Arrow

Scale in cm

Index Pointer

Liquid Filled Capsule

Magnetic Needle with Red Pointer

Bezel Ring

Clinometer

Figure 10-15: Floating Needle Compass.

Determining Direction of Travel:

Once you have determined your location on a map and the place you want to get to, and have plotted them, draw a straight line between the two positions. Use your compass to determine your azimuth, depicted below (see Figure 10-16).

This azimuth will be in relation to either geographic north (true north, represented by meridians of longitude), or grid north (north represented by the north/south running grid lines), both of which are different from the magnetic north that your compass needle points to. Remember the Declination diagram?

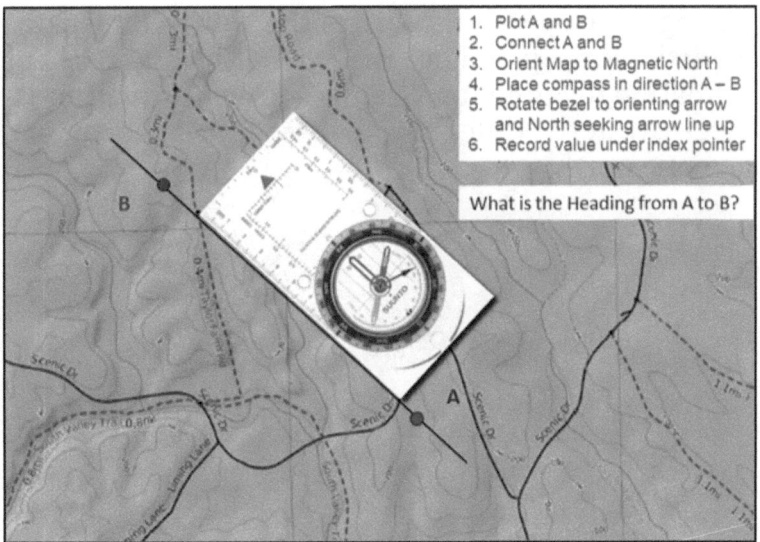

Figure 10-16: Determining Direction using a Magnetic Compass.

You will use this to determine the angular relationship between true, grid and magnetic north.

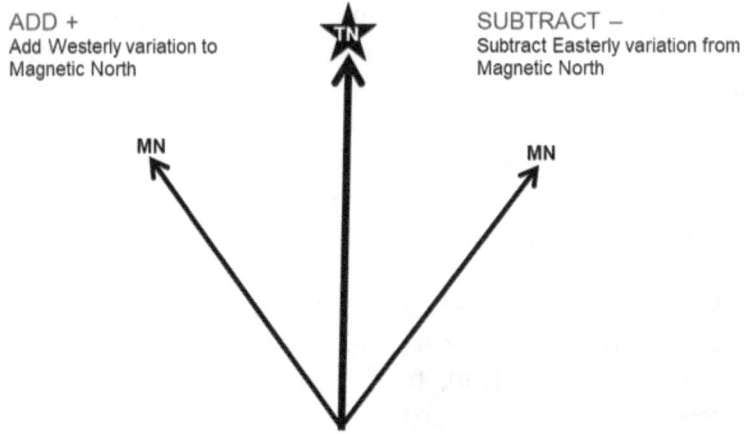

Figure 10-17: Declination Diagram.

Along the eastern seaboard of the United States, the magnetic north pole is to the west of true north. The declination diagram for Virginia (below) depicts an 11-degree westerly difference between true north and magnetic north:

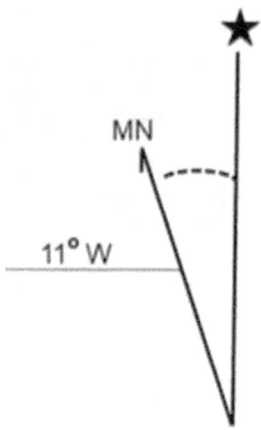

Figure 10-18: Virginia Declination.

In order to convert your grid azimuth to a magnetic azimuth you can follow on your compass, you must ADD 11 degrees.

Be aware that the magnetic north pole shifts over time, so consult the marginal data on your map to ensure it is up to date.

An alternate method to determine your azimuth is to place a protractor on the map, aligned with a north/south grid line, to determine the direction in degrees ("azimuth") from where you are to your destination.

Distance between points to be traveled is determined on a map using the bar scale (in the marginal data). Type of terrain that will be encountered along the route can be determined by interpreting contour lines and map symbols. Distance traveled on the ground is measured by pace count.

Pace count:

A pace is the distance covered every time the same foot touches the ground, generally measured over 100 meters (109.3613 yards). My pace count is roughly 62 paces to 100 meters, or 620 paces per kilometer. Pace count will vary according to terrain and conditions.

Estimate your pace count based on your terrain evaluation:

• **Relatively flat, level terrain**: 600-650 paces per kilometer.

• **Moderate terrain**: 800-850 paces per kilometer.

•**Steep, rugged terrain**: approximately 1000 paces per kilometer.

Certain conditions also affect pace count in the field, and you must allow for them by making adjustments:

• **Winds**: a head wind shortens the pace, a tail wind increases it.

• **Surfaces**: sand, gravel, mud, snow, etc. tend to shorten the pace.

• **Elements**: snow, rain, or ice will shorten your pace.

• **Clothing**: excess clothing and type footwear affect pace length.

• **Visibility**: poor visibility, such as in fog, rain, or darkness, will shorten your pace.

Do not try to remember the total pace count, you'll never keep track in your head. An effective method to keep track of distance traveled when using the pace count is to tie a knot in a string every 100 meters; when you get to ten knots, you've traveled 1 kilometer; but then you have to untie your knots while keeping track of your current pace in your head. My pace count cord is rubber grommets on paracord:

Figure 10-19: Pace Count Cord & Beads.

Time of arrival can be roughly estimated by assuming a walking speed (cross country over uneven terrain) of 1 kilometer per hour. As mentioned above, factors that may influence rate of travel include things such as physical condition, terrain, weather, etc. so adjust as necessary.

Bypassing obstacles:

A method to bypass obstacles and still stay on azimuth is to detour around the obstacle by moving at right angles for specified distances.

For example, while moving on an azimuth of 90° you encounter a large body of water and associated marshy terrain, depicted below (see Figure below).

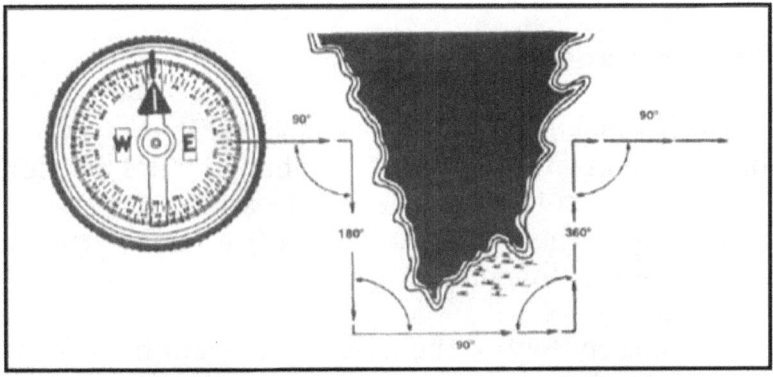

Figure 10-20: Bypassing obstacles using the Box Method.

To bypass this obstacle using the box method:

• Change your azimuth to 180° and travel for 100 meters.

• Change your azimuth to 90°and travel for 150 meters.

• Change your azimuth to 360°and travel for 100 meters.

• Then, change your azimuth to 90°and you are back on your original azimuth line.

Your magnetic compass can also keep you from getting lost, if following a trail or descending from high ground. Suppose you wish to go off-trail, perhaps to investigate the sound of water, or because nature calls. Consult your compass first, rotating the bezel to a direction 90° opposite your direction of travel on the trail. When you wish to return to the trail, simply change your azimuth 180° and follow your compass back to the trail.

Features and use of a GPS:

The Global Positioning System (GPS) is a space-based satellite navigation system that provides location and time information in all weather conditions, anywhere on the earth where there is an unobstructed line of sight to the horizon.

In the early 1970's, the U.S. Department of Defense (DoD) developed a robust, stable navigation system using satellites. DoD then followed through and launched its first Navigation System with Timing and Ranging (NAVSTAR) satellite in 1978. The 24 satellite system became fully operational in 1993.

Nowadays there are many types of GPS devices available for recreational and professional use. While they vary in size, type and quality, general rules of thumb for using a GPS are:

• Ensure device has clear line of sight to the sky; move as needed to improve quality strength.

• Dense foliage degrades signal (leaves are 90% water, and water blocks radio signal).

• Battery life; conserve battery life, be aware of power remaining, and plan on having a method to recharge or replace batteries.

• Once device has acquired satellites for positional fix, coordinates will be displayed automatically on the device's screen.

When reporting your position, be aware that a GPS may provide geo coordinates in three formats of latitude and longitude (as previously mentioned, above):

• Degrees-Minutes-Seconds (DMS): N 00°00'00.0", W 000°00'00.0"

• Degrees-Minutes-Decimal minutes (DMM or DDM): 00°00.000' N, 000°00.000' W

• Decimal Degrees (DDD or DD): 00.00000°, -000.00000°

GPS's also provide location in UTM, in many coordinate systems. The coordinate system for USNG / MGRS is WGS 84.

B. Celestial Navigation

There are several methods by which you can determine direction by the position in the sky of the sun and the stars. These methods, however, will give you only a general direction. You can come up with a more nearly true direction if you know the terrain of the region where you are going.

If possible, learn all you can about the terrain prior to your activity, especially any prominent features or landmarks. Knowledge of the terrain together with using the methods explained below will let you come up with fairly true directions to help you navigate.

I. Using the Sun and Shadows

The earth's relationship to the sun can help you to determine direction on earth. The sun always rises in the east and sets in the west, but not exactly due east or due west. There is also some seasonal variation. In the northern hemisphere, the sun will be due south when at its highest point in the sky, or when an object casts no appreciable shadow.

In the southern hemisphere, this same noonday sun will mark due north. In the northern hemisphere, shadows will move clockwise. Shadows will move counterclockwise in the southern hemisphere. With practice, you can use shadows to determine both direction and time of day. The shadow methods used for direction finding are the shadow-tip and watch methods (see Figures below).

Shadow-Tip Methods

In the first shadow-tip method, find a straight stick 1 meter long, and a level spot free of brush on which the stick will cast a definite shadow. This method is simple and accurate and consists of four steps:

1 Mark the shadow's tip.

2 Mark the new position and draw a line through the two marks.

3 Stand with the first mark to your left and the second mark to your right – you are now facing north.

Figure 10-21: Shadow-Tip Method for finding North.

Step 1: Place the stick or branch into the ground at a level spot where it will cast a distinctive shadow. Mark the shadow's tip with a stone, twig, or other means.

This first shadow mark is always west - everywhere on Earth.

Step 2: Wait 10 to 15 minutes until the shadow tip moves a few centimeters. Mark the shadow tip's new position in the same way as the first.

Step 3: Draw a straight line through the two marks to obtain an approximate east-west line.

Step 4: Stand with the first mark (west) to your left and the second mark to your right - you are now facing north. This fact is true everywhere on Earth.

An alternate method is more accurate but requires more time. Set up your shadow stick and mark the first shadow in the morning. Use a piece of string to draw a clean arc through this mark and around the stick. At midday, the shadow will shrink and disappear. In the afternoon, it will lengthen again and at the point where it touches the arc, make a second mark. Draw a line through the two marks to get an accurate east-west line.

The Watch Method

You can also determine direction using a common or analog watch (one that has hands). The direction will be accurate if you are using true local time, without any changes for daylight savings time. Remember, the further you are from the equator, the more accurate this method will be. If you only have a digital watch, you can overcome this obstacle. Quickly draw a watch on a circle of paper with the correct time on it and use it to determine your direction at that time.

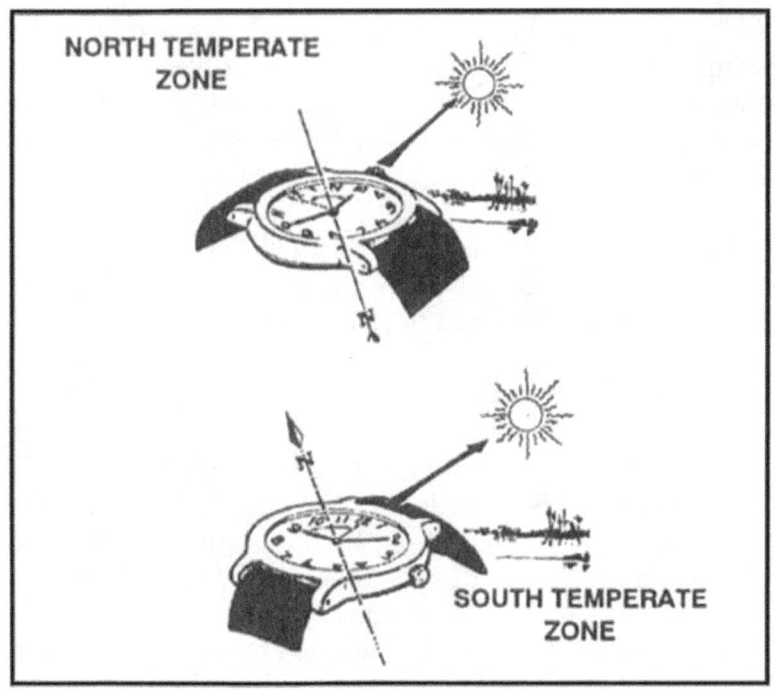

Figure 10-22: Watch Method.

In the northern hemisphere, hold the watch horizontal and point the hour hand at the sun. Bisect the angle between the hour hand and the 12 o'clock mark to get the north-south line (second figure). If there is any doubt as to which end of the line is north, remember that the sun rises in the east, sets in the west, and is due south at noon. The sun is in the east before noon and in the west after noon.

In the southern hemisphere, point the watch's 12 o'clock mark toward the sun and a midpoint halfway between 12 and the hour hand will give you the north-south line.

The watch method for finding north can also be used using a digital watch; this method involves drawing a picture of an analog watch with the hands depicting the current time, and aligning it with the sun as discussed above.

NOTE: If your watch is set on daylight savings time, use the midway point between the hour hand and 1 o'clock to determine the north-south line.

II. Using the Moon

Because the moon has no light of its own, we can only see it when it reflects the sun's light. As it orbits the earth on its 28-day circuit, the shape of the reflected light varies according to its position. We say there is a new moon or no moon when it is on the opposite side of the earth from the sun. Then, as it moves away from the earth's shadow, it begins to reflect light from its right side and waxes to become a full moon before waning, or losing shape, to appear as a sliver on the left side. You can use this information to identify direction.

If the moon rises before the sun has set, the illuminated side will be the west. If the moon rises after midnight, the illuminated side will be the east. This obvious discovery provides us with a rough east-west reference during the night.

III. Using the Stars

Your location in the Northern or Southern Hemisphere determines which constellation you use to determine your north or south direction.

The Northern Sky

The main constellations to learn are the Ursa Major, also known as the Big Dipper, and Cassiopeia (above). Neither of these constellations ever sets. They are always visible on a clear night.

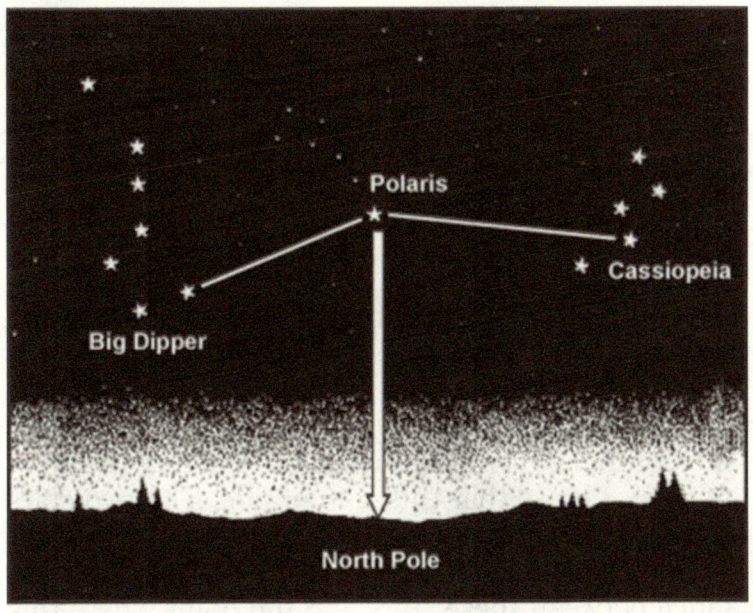

Figure 10-23: The Northern Sky.

Use them to locate Polaris, also known as the North Star. The North Star forms part of the Little Dipper handle and can be confused with the Big Dipper.

Prevent confusion by using both the Big Dipper and Cassiopeia together. The Big Dipper and Cassiopeia are always directly opposite each other and rotate counterclockwise around Polaris, with Polaris in the center. The Big Dipper is a seven-star constellation in the shape of a dipper. The two stars forming the outer lip of this dipper are the "pointer stars" because they point to the North Star. Mentally draw a line from the outer bottom star to the outer top star of the Big Dipper's bucket. Extend this line about five times the distance between the pointer stars. You will find the North Star along this line.

Cassiopeia has five stars that form a shape like a "W" on its side. The North Star is straight out from Cassiopeia's center star. After locating the North Star, locate the North Pole or true north by drawing an imaginary line directly downwards to the Earth.

The Southern Sky

Because there is no star bright enough to be easily recognized near the south celestial pole, a constellation known as the Southern Cross is used as a signpost to the South (below).

The Southern Cross has five stars. Its four brightest stars form a cross that tilts to one side. The two stars that make up the cross's long axis are the pointer stars. To determine south, imagine a distance five times the distance between these stars and the point where this imaginary line ends is in the general direction of south. Look down to the horizon from this imaginary point and select a landmark to steer by. In a static survival situation, you can fix this location in daylight if you drive stakes in the ground at night to point the way.

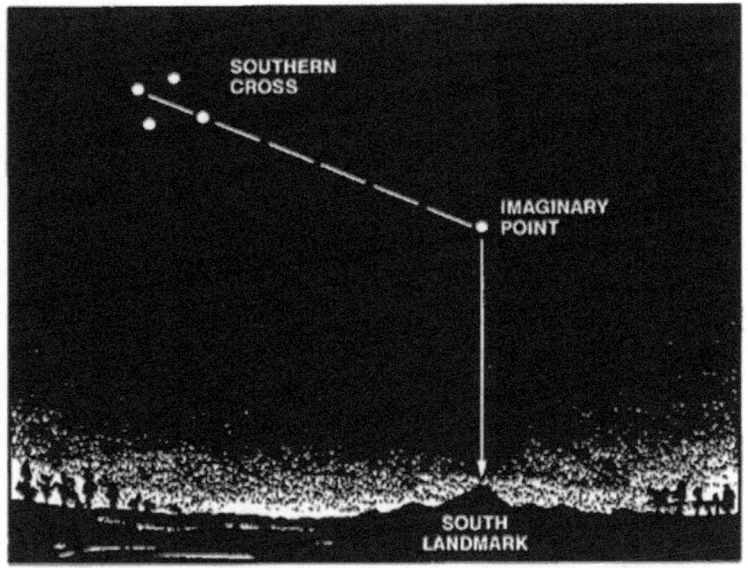

Figure 10-24: The Southern Sky.

C. Expedient Navigation & Miscellaneous Travel Methods

Movement also involves being able to move across country over uneven terrain – this requires footwear (preferably stout shoes) and perhaps a walking staff, which can double as a weapon against aggressive wildlife. Practice this skill and build up your muscles for it by hiking with a pack on your back.

The military standard for a road march is 12 miles in 3 hours (approximately 4 miles per hour) but this standard is for fit, trained soldiers moving on a road under ideal conditions.

Your physical state in a survival situation and the challenges of the terrain may slow you down to less than one half mile per hour. Take this into consideration as you plan your movement. In other words, is it realistic to expect that you can walk your way out of your situation, or can you go to a location suitable for making signal - as in the case of Karen Klein where her husband was able to move to higher ground to acquire cellphone signal to coordinate recovery, while Karen nearly perished during her attempt to reach help on foot. Is there water along your planned route – or, as in the case of Autumn Veatch, can you follow a water feature to civilization?

The US Army Field Manual 21-18 Foot Marches covers requirements for fundamentals of movement over terrain by foot; what the general population refers to as hiking or trekking.

FM 21-18 also discusses acclimatization, individual's loads, physical limitations and stress, and significantly, foot care.

"For the want of a nail the shoe was lost,
For the want of a shoe the horse was lost,
For the want of a horse the rider was lost,
For the want of a rider the battle was lost,
For the want of a battle the kingdom was lost,
And all for the want of a horseshoe nail."
— Benjamin Franklin

I. Foot Care

This maxim applies as much to humans as it does to horses. Poor fitting boots can cause blisters, and a bad blister will render the fittest, most conditioned hiker unable to walk (can even kill if it infects). Boots must be properly 'broken in', and attention must be paid to socks, insoles, and proper treatment of blisters. An improper fitted insole recently caused me to suffer a deep blood blister on my right heel that seriously limited my ability to walk for three days.

FM 21-18 presents preventative foot care guidance and basic treatment for blisters. To avoid painful foot problems, keep toenails trimmed short and square (straight across). Keep feet clean and dry and use foot powder. Wear clean, dry, well-fitting socks (preferably cushion-soled) inside-out (seams and knots on the outside).

The FM suggests wearing nylon or polypropylene sock liners but for long distance foot movement I personally advise against this; wearing two pairs of socks can create friction 'hotspots' that lead to blisters. Do carry an extra pair of socks, however, so you have a dry pair to change into. Carefully fit new boots; when 'breaking in' a new pair of boots, alternate with another pair.

If possible, tape known hot spots on your feet before setting out. During breaks (about ten minutes every hour when moving fast over even terrain), rest with your feet elevated on your rucksack. If time permits, remove your boots, rub your feet, apply foot powder, change socks, and treat blisters if necessary. Cover open blisters, cuts, or abrasions with absorbent adhesive bandages.

Common causes of blisters and abrasions are friction or pressure from improperly conditioned feet, ill-fitting footwear, and socks, improperly maintained footwear, heat, and moisture.

Obtain relief from swelling feet by slightly loosening bootlaces where they cross the arch of the foot. Inspect painful feet for blisters and abrasions from improper fitting of socks and boots.

Feet can develop red, swollen, tender skin along the sides of the feet from prolonged marching, which may become blisters. Keep your feet clean; the formation of blisters and abrasions with dirt and perspiration can cause infection, which in a survival situation can be lethal. If possible, wash your feet daily; cool water seems to reduce the sensation of heat and irritation.

To treat a blister, wash gently around it with soap and water, being careful not to break the skin. If unbroken, use a sterilized needle or knifepoint to prick the lower edge of the blister to remove fluid. (To sterilize needle or knifepoint, hold in a flame.)

If possible do not remove the skin; infection is a concern, so, if possible, apply antiseptic and/or antibiotic ointment (see Chapter 9. Medical Considerations, B. Primitive Medicine for alternate antiseptic treatments).

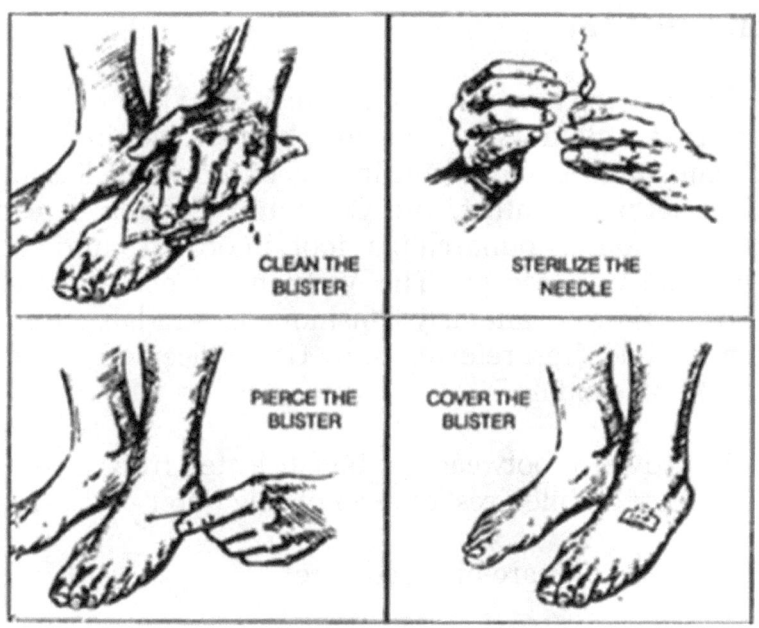

Figure 10-25: Treating Blisters

Cover the blister with an absorbent adhesive bandage or similar dressing, extending beyond the edge of the blister. After applying the dressing, dust the outside of the dressing and entire foot with foot powder.

Cover abrasions and cuts on the foot with absorbent adhesive bandages for rapid healing. Foot powder lessens friction on the skin and prevents the raw edges of the adhesive plaster from adhering to socks. The adhesive plaster should be smooth so it can serve as a "second skin." Check the blister periodically for proper drying. After the blister has dried, remove the adhesive plaster.

II. Footwear

For moving over uneven terrain, a good pair of boots or stout walking shoes are an absolute requirement. Circumstances may result in loss of footwear. During the Vietnam conflict, the Communists often forced their prisoners to march barefoot, in order to mitigate the ability to escape. The Vietnamese peasantry of those times famously fashioned sandals from automobile tires, referred to by US servicemen as "Ho Chi Minh sandals."

Improvised footwear can be fabricated from leather hide, automobile tires, or even plastic water bottles.

Some examples are pictured here:

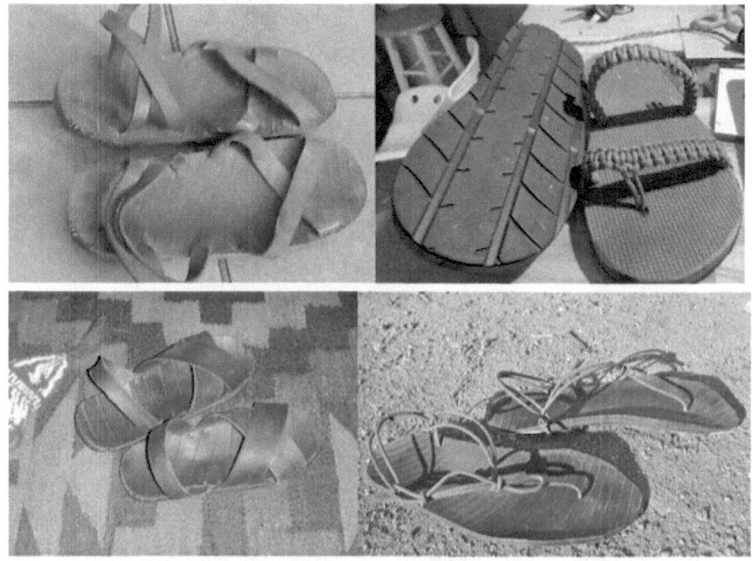

Figure 10-26: Improvised Footwear.

Figure 10-27: Improvised Footwear (continued).

For arctic or alpine conditions, requirements vary. Snow over-boots or mukluks can allow one to deal with extreme winter conditions in a pair of ordinary hiking boots or shoes.

Figure 10-28: Snow Over-Boots.

Snowshoes may be necessary – these may be commercial, military grade, or fabricated:

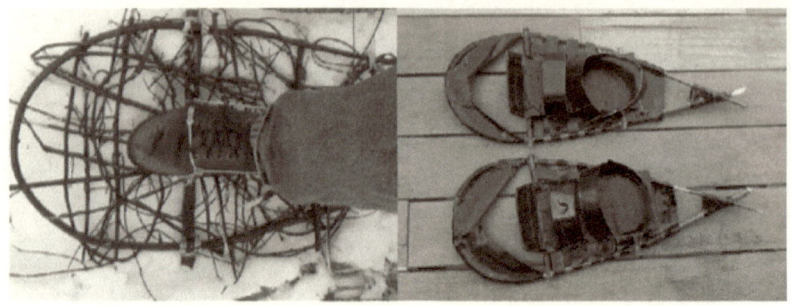

Figure 10-29: Improvised Snowshoes

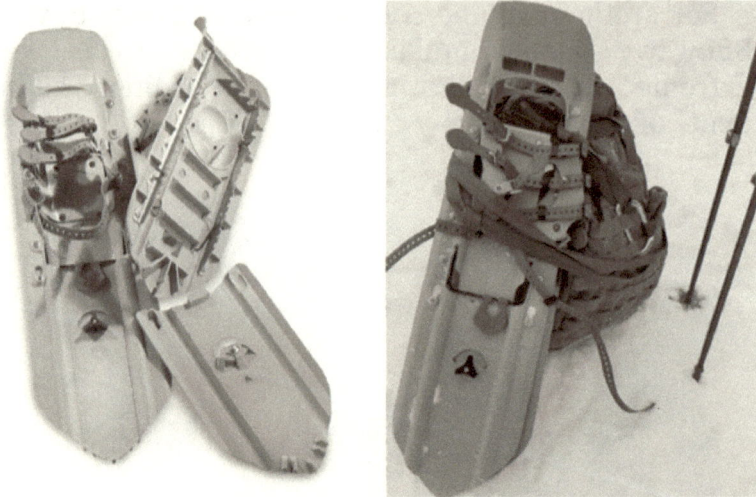

Figure 10-30: Military Snowshoes.

III. Travel Tips

Pinpoint your initial location as accurately as possible to determine a general line of travel to safety. If you do not have a compass, use a field-expedient direction-finding method. Move in one direction, but not necessarily in a straight line. Avoid obstacles. Take advantage of natural lines of drift.

A time proven technique for navigating out of the wilderness to civilization is to find a water feature, such as a small creek or a stream, and follow it. Human habitation - villages, towns and cities – occur along riverbanks. Be aware that the densest foliage occurs in the low ground where drainage creates these water features, and it may be necessary to move to higher ground to make progress. In doing so, maintain awareness of the location of the water feature in relation to where you are, as you follow it.

If you have survived an aircraft crash, secure important items from the crash site if possible; machete, compass, first aid kit, insect repellent, and a parachute or other material for use as mosquito netting and shelter. Do not leave the crash area without carefully blazing or marking your route. Use your compass. Know what direction you are taking.

IV. Travel through Jungle Areas

With practice, movement through thick undergrowth and jungle can be done efficiently. To move easily, you must develop "jungle eye"; look through the jungle, not at it. Do should not concentrate on the pattern of bushes and trees to your immediate front, instead must focus on the foliage further out and find natural breaks. Move smoothly through the jungle. Do not blunder through it since you will get many cuts and scratches. Turn your shoulders, shift your hips, bend your body, and shorten or lengthen your stride as necessary to slide between the undergrowth.

Stay alert and move slowly and steadily through dense forest or jungle. Stop periodically to listen and take your bearings. If you use a machete to cut through dense vegetation, do not cut unnecessarily or you will quickly wear yourself out. As much as possible use your machete or a stick to part the vegetation. Using a stick will also help dislodge biting ants, spiders, or snakes. Do not grasp at brush or vines when climbing slopes; they may have irritating spines or sharp thorns.

Promptly treat any wound, no matter how minor. In the tropics, even the smallest scratch can quickly become dangerously infected. Long sleeved shirts and trousers help to avoid cuts and scratches.

Many jungle and forest animals follow game trails. Stop and stoop down occasionally to look along the jungle floor; this may reveal game trails that you can follow. These trails wind and cross, but frequently lead to water or clearings. Use these trails if they lead in your desired direction of travel.

In many countries, electric and telephone lines run for miles through sparsely inhabited areas. Usually, the right-of-way is clear enough to allow easy travel.

Immediate Considerations

Because there is less likelihood of rescue from beneath a dense jungle canopy than in other survival situations, you will probably have to travel to reach safety.

Take shelter from tropical rain, sun, and insects. Malaria-carrying mosquitoes and other insects are immediate dangers, so protect yourself against bites.

V. Travel in Arctic and/or Alpine Areas, or Temperate Zone Winter Conditions

Survival and movement in an arctic or subarctic region presents many challenges. Location and the time of the year will determine the types of obstacles and the inherent dangers.

One should:

• Avoid traveling during a blizzard.

• Take care when crossing thin ice. Distribute your weight by lying flat and crawling.

• Cross streams when the water level is lowest. Normal freezing and thawing action may cause a stream level to vary as much as 2 to 2.5 meters per day. This variance may occur any time during the day, depending on the distance from a glacier, the temperature, and the terrain. Consider this variation in water level when selecting a campsite near a stream.

• Consider the clear arctic air. It makes estimating distance difficult. You more frequently underestimate than overestimate distances.

• Do not travel in "whiteout" conditions. The lack of contrasting colors makes it impossible to judge the nature of the terrain.

• Always cross a snow bridge at right angles to the obstacle it crosses. Find the strongest part of the bridge by poking ahead of you with a pole or ice axe. Distribute your weight by crawling or by wearing snowshoes or skis.

• Make camp early so that you have plenty of time to build a shelter.

• Consider frozen or unfrozen rivers as avenues of travel. However, some rivers that appear frozen may have soft, open areas that make travel very difficult or may not allow walking, skiing, or sledding.

• Use snowshoes if you are traveling over snow-covered terrain. Snow 30 or more centimeters deep makes traveling difficult.

• If you do not have snowshoes, make a pair using willow, strips of cloth, leather, or other suitable material.

It is almost impossible to travel in deep snow without snowshoes or skis. If you must travel in deep snow, avoid snow-covered streams.

The snow, which acts as an insulator, may have prevented ice from forming over the water. In hilly terrain, avoid areas where avalanches appear possible. Travel in the early morning in areas where there is danger of avalanches. On ridges, snow gathers on the lee side in overhanging piles called cornices.

These often extend far out from the ridge and may break loose if stepped on.

VI. Water Crossings

In a survival situation, you may have to cross a water obstacle such as a river, a stream, a lake, a bog, quicksand, quagmire, or muskeg. In the desert, flash floods occur, making streams an obstacle. Whatever it is, you need to know how to cross it safely.

Rivers and Streams: You can apply almost every description to rivers and streams. They may be shallow or deep, slow or fast moving, narrow or wide. Before you try to cross a river or stream, develop a good plan. Your first step is to look for a high place from which you can get a good view of the river or stream. From this place, you can look for a place to cross. If there is no high place, climb a tree.

Good crossing locations include:

• A level stretch where it breaks into several channels. Two or three narrow channels are usually easier to cross than a wide river.

• A shallow bank or sandbar. If possible, select a point upstream from the bank or sandbar so that the current will carry you to it if you lose your footing.

• A course across the river that leads downstream so that you will cross the current at about a 45-degree angle.

The following areas possess potential hazards; avoid them, if possible:

• Obstacles on the opposite side of the river that might hinder your travel. Try to select the spot from which travel will be the safest and easiest.

• A ledge of rocks that crosses the river. This often indicates dangerous rapids or canyons.

• A deep or rapid waterfall or a deep channel. Never try to ford a stream directly above or even close to such hazards.

• Rocky places. You may sustain serious injuries from slipping or falling on rocks. Usually, submerged rocks are very slick, making balance extremely difficult. An occasional rock that breaks the current, however, may help you.

•An estuary of a river. An estuary is normally wide, has strong currents, and is subject to tides. These tides can influence some rivers many kilometers from their mouths. Go back upstream to an easier crossing site.

• Eddies. An eddy can produce a powerful backward pull downstream of the obstruction causing the eddy and pull you under the surface.

The depth of a fordable river or stream is no deterrent if you can keep your footing. In fact, deep water sometimes runs more slowly and is therefore safer than fast-moving shallow water. You can always dry your clothes later, or if necessary, you can make a raft to carry your clothing and equipment across the river.

You must not try to swim or wade across a stream or river when the water is at very low temperatures. This swim could be fatal. Try to make a raft of some type. Wade across if you can get only your feet wet. Dry them vigorously as soon as you reach the other bank.

Improvised Rafts: A good reason for packing two ponchos and/or tarps, is that you can construct a brush raft or a poncho raft. If constructed correctly with a focus on waterproofing, it is possible float yourself and equipment across a slow-moving stream or river with either of these rafts.

Brush Raft: The brush raft, if properly constructed, will support about 115 kilograms.

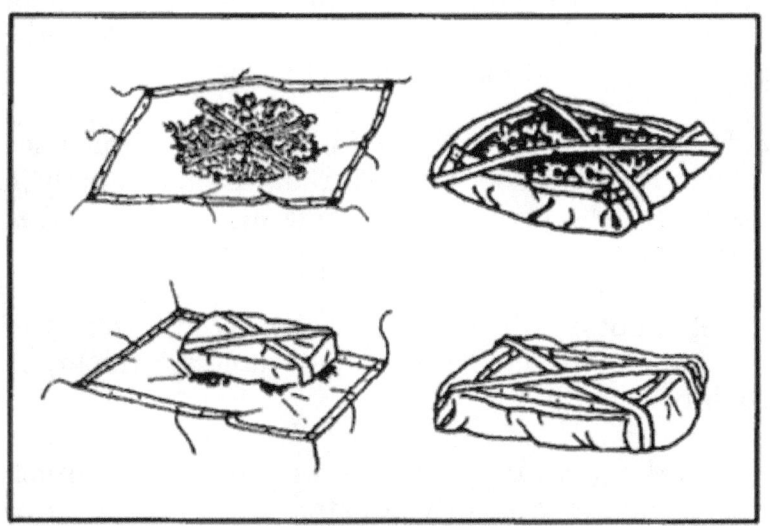

Figure 10-31: Brush Raft.

To construct a brush raft, use ponchos and/or tarps, fresh green brush, two small saplings, and rope or vine as follows:

1. If using a poncho, push the hood to the inner side and tightly tie off the necks using the drawstrings.

2. Attach paracord or other cord (or cordage fabricated from vines) at the corner and side grommets of each poncho or tarp. Make sure they are long enough to cross to and tie with the others attached at the opposite corner or side.

3. Spread one poncho or tarp on the ground with the inner side up. Pile fresh, green brush (no thick branches) on the poncho until the brush stack is about 18 inches (about 45 centimeters) high. Pull the drawstring up through the center of the brush stack.

4. Make an X-frame from two small saplings and place it on top of the brush stack. Tie the X-frame securely in place with the poncho drawstring, paracord or other cord.

5. Pile another 18 inches (about 45 centimeters) of brush on top of the X-frame, then compress the brush slightly.

6. Pull the poncho or tarp sides up around the brush and, using the cords or vines attached to the comer or side grommets, tie them diagonally from corner to corner and from side to side.

7. Spread the second poncho or tarp, inner side up, next to the brush bundle.

8. Roll the brush bundle onto the second poncho or tarp so that the tied side is down. Tie the second poncho or tarp around the brush bundle in the same manner as you tied the first poncho around the brush.

9. Place it in the water with the tied side of the second poncho or tarp facing up.

Poncho Raft: If you do not have time to gather brush for a brush raft, you can make a poncho raft using ponchos and/or tarps and your rucksack or backpack. This raft, although more waterproof than the poncho brush raft, will only float about 75 pounds (about 34 kilograms) of equipment. It is also important to have the contents of your rucksack or backpack waterproofed in as heavy-duty waterproof bags as possible, for floatation purposes.

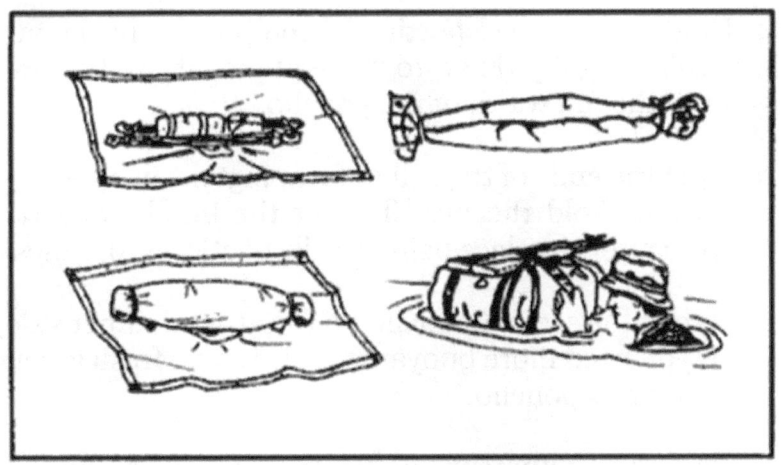

Figure 10-32: Poncho Raft.

To construct a poncho raft, use two ponchos and/or tarps, one or two rucksacks, two 1.2-meter poles or branches, and ropes, vines, bootlaces, or comparable material as follows:

1. Push the hood of each poncho to the inner side and tightly tie off the necks using the drawstrings.

2. Spread one poncho on the ground with the inner side up. Place and center the two 4 foot (1.2 meter) poles on the poncho about 18 inches (approximately 45 centimeters) apart.

3. Place your rucksacks, packs or other equipment between the poles. Also place other items that you want to keep dry between the poles. Snap the poncho sides together.

4. Hold the snapped portion of the poncho in the air and roll it tightly down to the equipment. Make sure you roll the full width of the poncho.

5. Twist the ends of the roll to form pigtails in opposite directions. Fold the pigtails over the bundle and tie them securely in place using cords, bootlaces, or vines.

6. Spread the second poncho on the ground, inner side up. If you need more buoyancy, place some fresh green brush on this poncho.

7. Place the equipment bundle, tied side down, on the center of the second poncho. Wrap the second poncho around the equipment bundle following the same procedure you used for wrapping the equipment in the first poncho.

8. Tie cords, bootlaces, vines, or other binding material around the raft about 12 inches (or 30 centimeters) from the end of each pigtail.

Rapids: If necessary, you can safely cross a deep, swift river or rapids. To swim across a deep, swift river, swim with the current, never fight it. Try to keep your body horizontal to the water. This will reduce the danger of being pulled under.

In fast, shallow rapids, lie on your back, feet pointing downstream, finning your hands alongside your hips. This action will increase buoyancy and help you steer away from obstacles. Keep your feet up to avoid getting them bruised or caught by rocks.

In deep rapids, lie on your stomach, head downstream, angling toward the shore whenever you can. Watch for obstacles and be careful of backwater eddies and converging currents, as they often contain dangerous swirls. Converging currents occur where new watercourses enter the river or where water has been diverted around large obstacles such as small islands.

To ford a swift, treacherous stream, apply the following steps:

• Remove your pants and shirt to lessen the water's pull on you. Keep your footgear on to protect your feet and ankles from rocks. It will also provide you with firmer footing.

• Tie your pants and other articles to the top of your rucksack or in a bundle, if you have no pack. This way, if you have to release your equipment, all your articles will be together. It is easier to find one large pack than to find several small items.

• Carry your pack well up on your shoulders and be sure you can easily remove it, if necessary. Not being able to get a pack off quickly enough can drag even the strongest swimmers under.

Find a strong pole about 7.5 centimeters in diameter and 2.1 to 2.4 meters long to help you ford the stream. Grasp the pole and plant it firmly on your upstream side to break the current. Plant your feet firmly with each step, and move the pole forward a little downstream from its previous position, but still upstream from you. With your next step, place your foot below the pole. Keep the pole well slanted so that the force of the current keeps the pole against your shoulder.

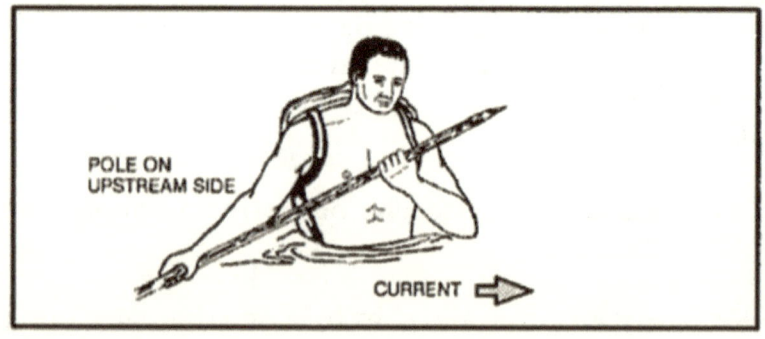

Figure 10-33: One Man Crossing a Swift Stream.

Cross the stream so that you will cross the downstream current at a 45-degree angle. Using this method, you can safely cross currents usually too strong for one person to stand against. Do not concern yourself about your pack's weight, as the weight will help rather than hinder you in fording the stream.

If there are other people with you, cross the stream together. Ensure that everyone has prepared their pack and clothing as outlined above. Position the heaviest person on the downstream end of the pole and the lightest on the upstream end. In using this method, the upstream person breaks the current, and those below can move with relative ease in the eddy formed by the upstream person. If the upstream person gets temporarily swept off his feet, the others can hold steady while he regains his footing, as shown below.

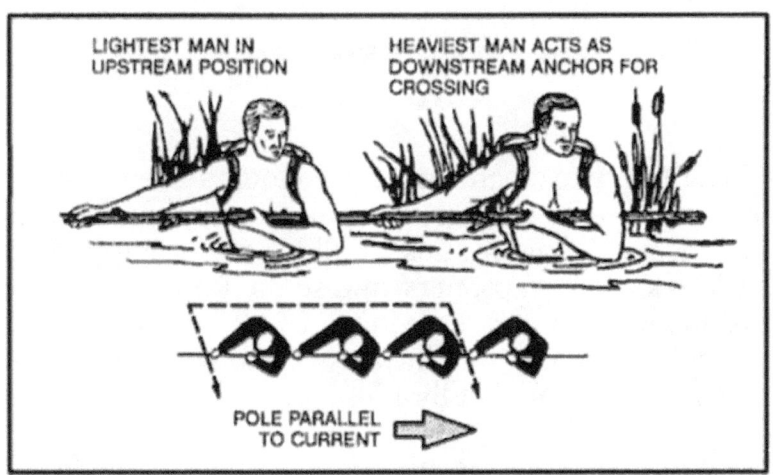

Figure 10-34: Several Men Crossing a Swift Stream.

11

Primitive or Improvised Weapons and Tools

The ability to create improvised tools and equipment is a vital skill in any survival situation. Examples include rope, digging sticks, walking sticks, improvised rucksacks, fish traps, nets, and so on. Rope or cordage fashioned from grasses, vines or even animal hide is possibly the most versatile piece of survival equipment, considering an almost limitless use.

By weapon, the meaning is a weapon suitable for hunting and dispatching small game. I have purposely not included information regarding crafting stone tools in this book. This skill set belongs in long-term survival, whereas the focus of this book concerns dealing with the immediate aftereffects of being thrust into a survival situation and getting out of it sooner than later. Knapping arrowheads, stone ax heads and stone knives is a skill that takes a lot of practice to successfully achieve results. Some people do it as a hobby; I once saw a guy make an impressive arrowhead out of the thick glass bottom of a coke bottle, but of course I haven't seen a coke bottle in over a decade. Part of the reason I do not include these skills in my writings is that I have never personally done this. Perhaps I will include a section on this subject in a future edition, but only after I have achieved results myself.

A. Knives

A knife may be your most valuable tool in a survival situation, along with the means to keep it sharp. Nothing is more useless than a dull knife. Lacking a sharpening stone or steel, a knife blade may be sharpened to a razor edge using flat rock or cement, or even the back of a ceramic plate.

It is possible that, due to local restrictions, you may be without a full-sized field knife. In this case, a smaller pocketknife or one of the modern multi-tools which include knife and saw blades, can be useful. With proper knowledge and skills, one can easily improvise a larger edged weapon from miscellaneous pieces of metal, stone, broken glass, bone or even wood.

My preferred field knife is the world-famous kukri carried by soldiers of the Gurkha regiments. This multipurpose blade is halfway between a machete and a hatchet, but due to its length is often illegal to carry openly, or even to possess in some overseas locations.

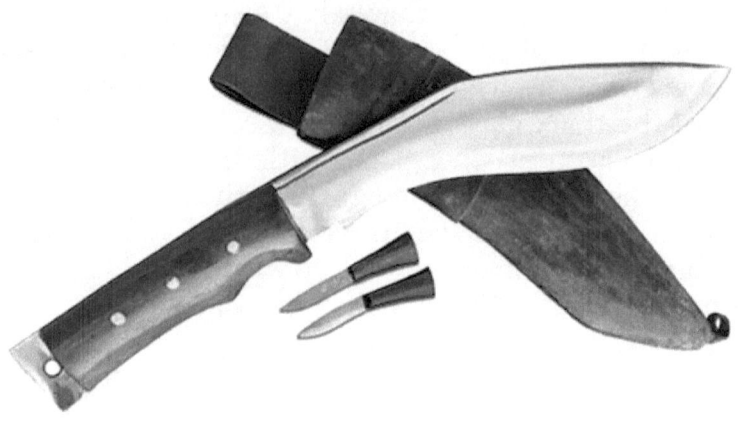

Figure 11-1: Kukri.

The US Air Force survival knife has been around for many years. This knife is not a frontiersman or bushcraft knife, per se; but its relatively small size and many features make it an extremely versatile, lightweight multi-purpose tool.

This knife consists of a metal blade with a saw-toothed spine, a leather grip, riveted butt plate, a handguard with two holes to modify into an improvised spear, a leather sheath with a pocket containing sharpening stone and a metal sheath protector to prevent the tip of the knife from penetrating the bottom of the sheath. The cutting blade is 5 1/8 inches long and 3/16 inches thick. The heavy octagonal butt plate may serve as a hammer.

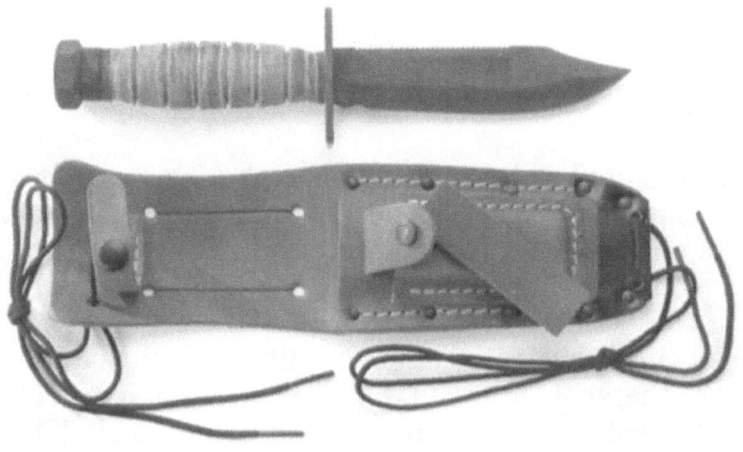

Figure 11-2: US Air Force Survival Knife

A. Improvised Weapons

I. Clubs

You hold clubs, you do not throw them. As a field-expedient weapon, the club does not protect you from enemy soldiers. It can, however, extend your area of defense beyond your fingertips. It also serves to increase the force of a blow without injuring yourself. There are three basic types of clubs. They are the simple, weighted, and sling club.

Simple Club

A simple club is a staff or branch. It must be short enough for you to swing easily, but long enough and strong enough for you to damage whatever you hit. Its diameter should fit comfortably in your palm, but it should not be so thin as to allow the club to break easily

251

upon impact. A straight-grained hardwood is best if you can find it.

Weighted Club

A weighted club is any simple club with a weight on one end. The weight may be a natural weight, such as a knot on the wood, or something added, such as a stone lashed to the club.

To make a weighted club, first find a stone that has a shape that will allow you to lash it securely to the club. A stone with a slight hourglass shape works well. If you cannot find a suitably shaped stone, you must fashion a groove or channel into the stone by a technique known as pecking. By repeatedly rapping the club stone with a smaller hard stone, you can get the desired shape.

Next, find a piece of wood that is the right length for you. A straight-grained hardwood is best. The length of the wood should feel comfortable in relation to the weight of the stone. Finally, lash the stone to the handle.

There are three techniques for lashing the stone to the handle: split handle, forked branch, and wrapped handle. The technique you use will depend on the type of handle you choose.

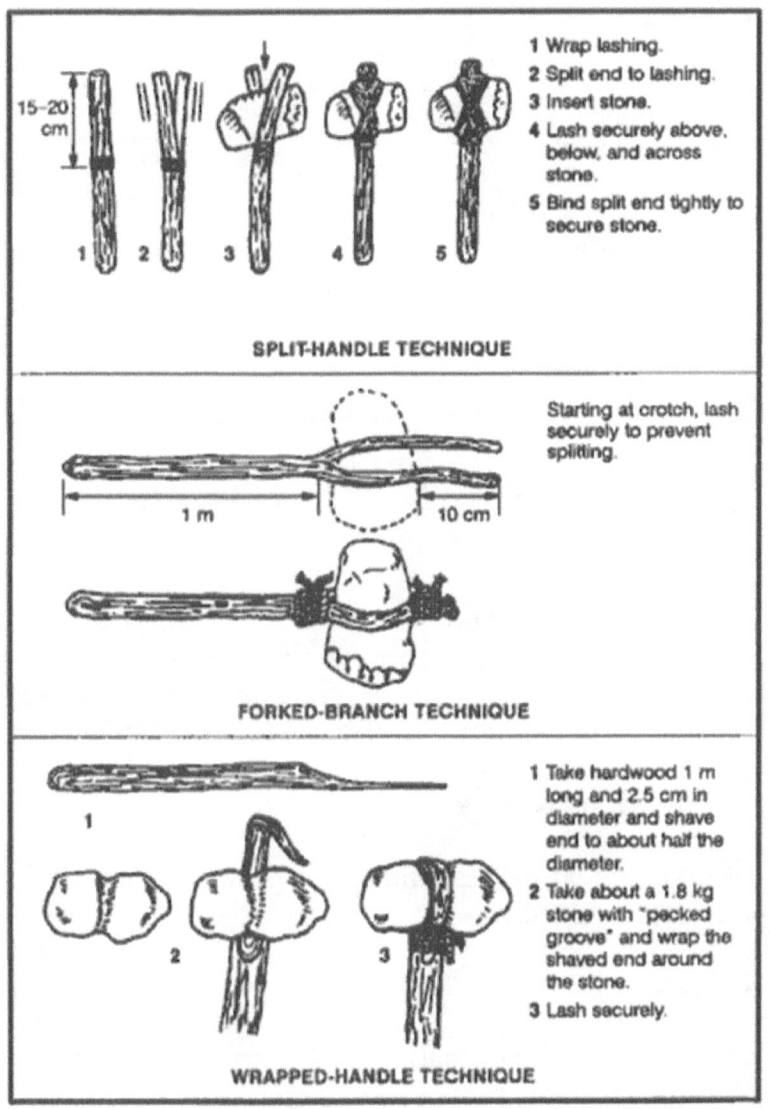

SPLIT-HANDLE TECHNIQUE

1 Wrap lashing.
2 Split end to lashing.
3 Insert stone.
4 Lash securely above, below, and across stone.
5 Bind split end tightly to secure stone.

FORKED-BRANCH TECHNIQUE

Starting at crotch, lash securely to prevent splitting.

WRAPPED-HANDLE TECHNIQUE

1 Take hardwood 1 m long and 2.5 cm in diameter and shave end to about half the diameter.
2 Take about a 1.8 kg stone with "pecked groove" and wrap the shaved end around the stone.
3 Lash securely.

Figure 11-3: Primitive Weapons - Lashing Clubs.

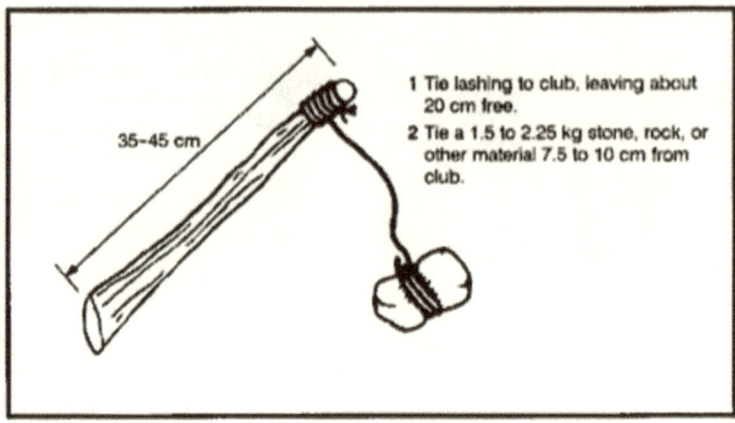

Figure 11-4: Sling Club.

Sling Club

A sling club is another type of weighted club. A weight hangs 8 to 10 centimeters from the handle by a strong, flexible lashing. This type of club both extends the user's reach and multiplies the force of the blow.

II. Edged Weapons

Knives, spear blades, and arrow points fall under the category of edged weapons.

Knives

Knives puncture, slash or chop, and cut. A knife is also an invaluable tool used to construct other survival items. An improvised knife, arrow heads or spear blades can be fabricated from stone, bone, wood, or metal.

Bone

You can also use bone as an effective field-expedient edged weapon. First, you will need to select a suitable bone. The larger bones, such as the leg bone of a deer or another medium-sized animal, are best. Lay the bone upon another hard object. Shatter the bone by hitting it with a heavy object, such as a rock. From the pieces, select a suitable pointed splinter.

You can further shape and sharpen this splinter by rubbing it on a rough-surfaced rock. If the piece is too small to handle, you can still use it by adding a handle to it. Select a suitable piece of hardwood for a handle and lash the bone splinter securely to it.

NOTE: A bone knife is used only to puncture. It will not hold an edge and it may flake or break if used differently.

Wood

You can make field-expedient edged weapons from wood. Use these only to puncture. Bamboo is the only wood that will hold a suitable edge. To make a knife using wood, first select a straight-grained piece of hardwood that is about 30 centimeters long and 2.5 centimeters in diameter. Fashion the blade about 15 centimeters long. Shave it down to a point. Use only the straight-grained portions of the wood. Do not use the core or pith, as it would make a weak point.

Harden the point by a process known as fire hardening. If a fire is possible, dry the blade portion over the fire slowly until lightly charred. The drier the wood, the harder the point. After lightly charring the blade portion, sharpen it on a coarse stone. If using bamboo and after fashioning the blade, remove any other wood to make the blade thinner from the inside portion of the bamboo. Removal is done this way because bamboo's hardest part is its outer layer. Keep as much of this layer as possible to ensure the hardest blade possible. When charring bamboo over a fire, char only the inside wood; do not char the outside.

Metal

Metal is the best material to make field-expedient edged weapons. Metal, when properly designed, can fulfill a knife's three uses--puncture, slice or chop, and cut. First, select a suitable piece of metal, one that most resembles the desired end product. Depending on the size and original shape, you can obtain a point and cutting edge by rubbing the metal on a rough-surfaced stone. If the metal is soft enough, you can hammer out one edge while the metal is cold. Use a suitable flat, hard surface as an anvil and a smaller, harder object of stone or metal as a hammer to hammer out the edge. Make a knife handle from wood, bone, or other material that will protect your hand.

Other Materials

You can use other materials to produce edged weapons. Glass is a good alternative to an edged weapon or tool, if no other material is available. Obtain a suitable piece in the same manner as described for bone. Glass has a natural edge but is less durable for heavy work. You can also sharpen plastic - if it is thick enough or hard enough - into a durable point for puncturing.

Spear Blades

To make spears, use the same procedures to make the blade that you used to make a knife blade. Then select a shaft (a straight sapling) 1.2 to 1.5 meters long. The length should allow you to handle the spear easily and effectively. Attach the spear blade to the shaft using lashing. The preferred method is to split the handle, insert the blade, then wrap or lash it tightly.

You can use other materials without adding a blade. Select a 1.2-to 1.5-meter-long straight hardwood shaft and shave one end to a point. If possible, fire harden the point. Bamboo also makes an excellent spear. Select a piece 1.2 to 1.5 meters long. Starting 8 to 10 centimeters back from the end used as the point, shave down the end at a 45-degree angle. Remember, to sharpen the edges, shave only the inner portion

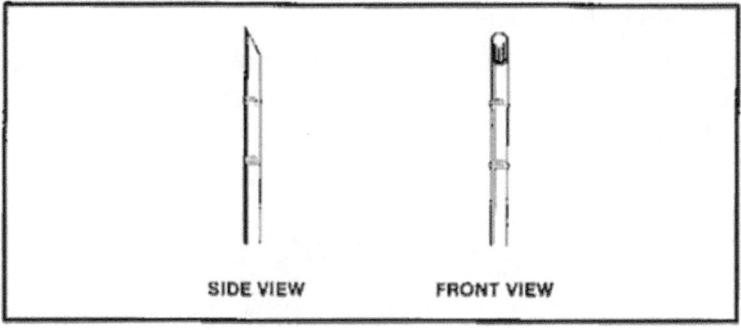

SIDE VIEW   FRONT VIEW

Figure 11-5. Bamboo Spear.

III. Other Expedient Weapons

You can make other field-expedient weapons such as the throwing stick, archery equipment, and the bolo.

Throwing Stick

The throwing stick, commonly known as the rabbit stick, is very effective against small game (squirrels, chipmunks, and rabbits). The rabbit stick itself is a blunt stick, naturally curved at about a 45-degree angle. Select a stick with the desired angle from heavy hardwood such as oak. Shave off two opposite sides so that the stick is flat like a boomerang. You must practice the throwing technique for accuracy and speed.

First, align the target by extending the non-throwing arm in line with the mid to lower section of the target. Slowly and repeatedly raise the throwing arm up and back until the throwing stick crosses the back at about a 45-degree angle or is in line with the non-throwing hip. Bring the throwing arm forward until it is just slightly above and parallel to the non-throwing arm. This will be the throwing stick's release point. Practice slowly and repeatedly to attain accuracy.

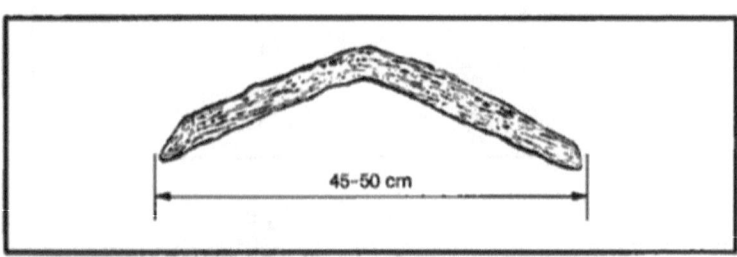

45-50 cm

Figure 11-6: Throwing Stick or "Rabbit Stick."

Bow and Arrow

A good bow requires many hours of work. Select a hardwood stick about one meter long that is free of knots or limbs; type of wood is not important. Carefully scrape the large end down until it has the same pull as the small end. Careful examination will show the natural curve of the stick. Always scrape from the side that faces you, or the bow will break the first time you pull it. Dead, dry wood is preferable to green wood. The bowstring can be any type of cordage. Tie the bowstring from one end of the bow to the other, without any slack. Select arrows from the straightest dry sticks available.

The arrows should be about half as long as the bow. Scrape each shaft smooth all around. You will probably have to straighten the shaft. You can bend an arrow straight by heating the shaft over hot coals. Do not allow the shaft to scorch or bum. Hold the shaft straight until it cools.

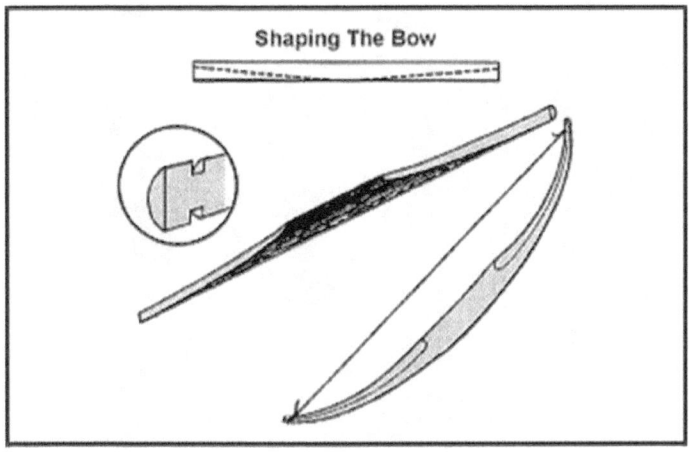

Figure 11-7: Primitive Weapons – Bow.

Arrowheads can be fabricated from bone, glass, metal, or pieces of rock. You can also sharpen and fire-harden the end of the shaft. To fire harden wood, hold it over hot coals, being careful not to burn or scorch the wood.

The ends of the arrows must be notched for the bowstring. Cut or file the notch; do not split it. Fletching (adding feathers to the notched end of an arrow) improves the arrow's flight characteristics but is not necessary on a field-expedient arrow.

Bolo

The bolo is another field-expedient weapon that is easy to make and is especially effective for capturing running game or low-flying fowl in a flock. To use the bola, hold it by the center knot and twirl it above your head. Release the knot so that the bola flies toward your target. When you release the bolo, the weighted cords will separate. These cords will wrap around and immobilize the fowl or animal that you hit.

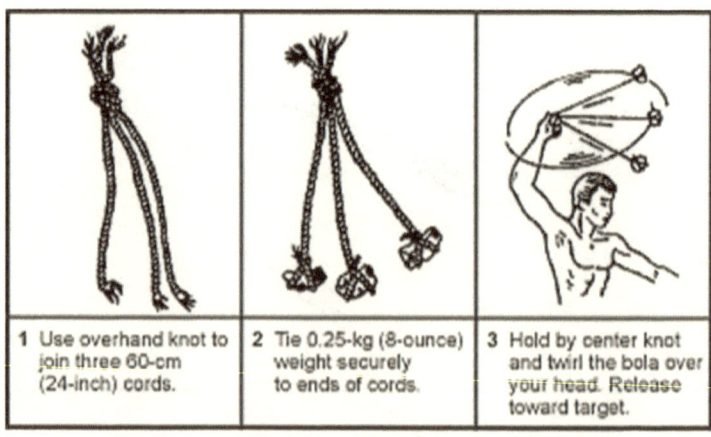

| 1 Use overhand knot to join three 60-cm (24-inch) cords. | 2 Tie 0.25-kg (8-ounce) weight securely to ends of cords. | 3 Hold by center knot and twirl the bola over your head. Release toward target. |

Figure 11-8: Bolo.

IV. Motor Vehicles

Motor vehicles are so ubiquitous in our modern world that it would be remiss not to include them. In my opinion, the perfect survival kit container - given that size is not a constraint - is a diesel truck, around the half ton size. Motor vehicles are also machines that have killed more people than the atom bomb. The letter "I" for Improvise in Keyword S.U.R.V.I.V.A.L. applies in both cases.

In using a vehicle as a weapon against bad actors, forcing your way through a crowd or ramming through roadblocks, there are some considerations:

• Be aware that airbag sensors may be mounted in the middle of your front end, right in front of the radiator.

• Be aware that front quarter panels can absorb more damage than your radiator – a vehicle with a damaged radiator will not go far.

Given the above considerations, if you must ram vehicles being used as improvised roadblocks, attempt to impact off center. The desired point of impact is the rear wheel of the roadblock vehicle (see figure below).

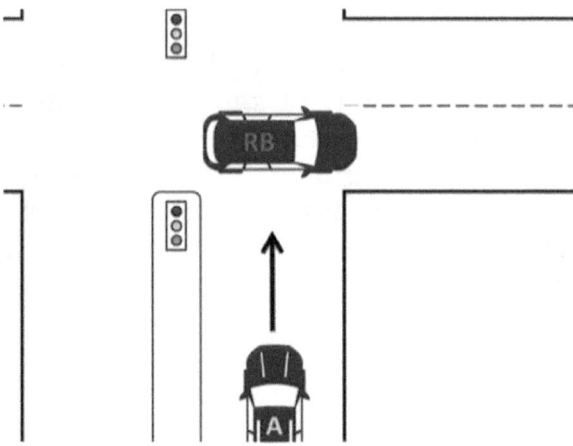

Figure 11-9: Vehicle vs Improvised Roadblock.

RB represents a vehicle being used as an improvised roadblock. Driver A is cut off as he/she enters the intersection (arrow indicates direction of travel). There is a traffic island in the middle of the roadway. Driver A accelerates and aims to impact RB at rear wheel:

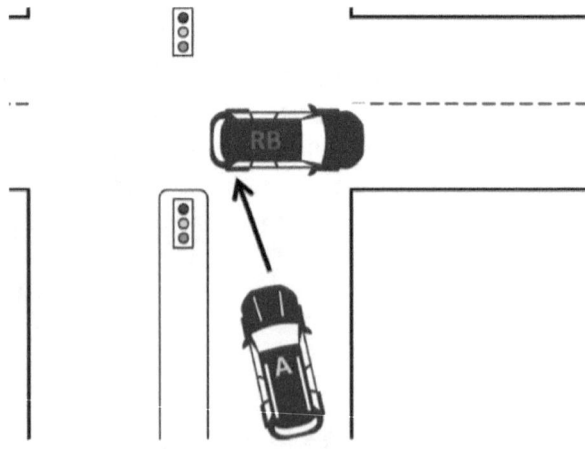

Figure 11-10: Vehicle vs Improvised Roadblock.

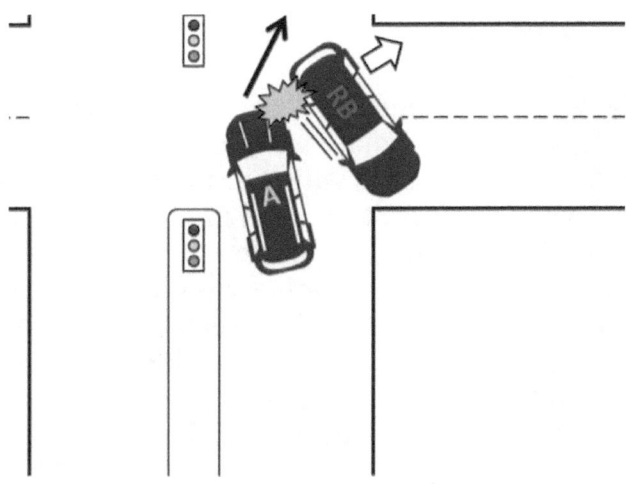

Figure 11-11: Vehicle vs Improvised Roadblock.

Driver A impacts RB vehicle at rear wheel; RB vehicle slides out of way (engine weight acts as a pivot point). Driver A departs.

CAUTION: If forced to execute such a maneuver, or to otherwise use your vehicle as a weapon, consider your operational environment; for overseas destinations – depending on where you are – consider seeking guidance from your embassy before reporting to local law enforcement, if this is practical. Otherwise, report the situation to law enforcement and seek legal guidance.

A final note: the advantage of being in a vehicle is that you can avoid negative encounters by simple driving away, and this should be your primary course of action at all times.

V. Combatives

A General officer once told a group I was part of that our bodies are our ultimate weapon, and one day come it may come down to you will have to fight for your life. Of course, the best way to prevail in this kind of fight is to not be there in the first place – I studiously avoid putting myself into challenging circumstances. Given that this may not be an option, seek training in close personal combat. The following guidance is from a good friend and fellow SERE instructor, who like myself, trains people in survival skills:

How to Win a Fight

You don't need fancy techniques, gold medals or 5 black belts:

1. Recognize pre-assault indicators.

2. Beat your opponent mentally by being first to make a decision and have a plan.

3. Don't worry about what you think they can do. Know what you're going to do instead and be committed.

4. Control distance/range and use it to your advantage.

5. Understand that action is faster than reaction.

CAVEAT: The above guidance addresses attitude and élan, but it does not replace training and a repertoire of good moves.

Another colleague once described a confrontation he found himself in; his opening move was a leg sweep – it's a good move but I suggest some training – the battle quickly resulted in his opponent on the ground getting his face kicked in.

The words of General George S. Patton come to mind:

"The only thing to do when a son-of-a-bitch looks cross-eyed at you is to beat the hell out of him right then and there."

General Patton's guidance is to recognize pre-assault indicators and be the first to engage; the one who gets there "firstest with the mostest" wins.

11: Primitive or Improvised Weapons and Tools

The best advice is to avoid any kind of violence to the greatest extent possible, of course, and to have well thought-out courses of action for if and when unavoidable circumstances present themselves.

12

Miscellaneous Survival Tips

Survival is 80 percent attitude, 10 percent equipment and 10 percent skill and knowledge.

Always carry a survival kit and know how to use it. A survival kit's contents should include items from the following categories: shelter, water (the means to procure it, filter and purify it, and transport and store it), food (the means to procure it, prepare and preserve it), signaling, medicine, weapon or tool (or the means to create a weapon or tool), and movement/navigation. Examples include a knife, fire starter items, compass, reflective survival blanket, high-energy food, water purification tablets, trauma first aid items, and signal items such as a mirror, whistle, flares and a Personal Locator Beacon (PLB).

I. High-Altitude Survival:

Every year more than a few hunters must be rescued from the wilds and high country; trapped by snowstorms, injured in various types of accidents or simply lost in the woods.

Altitude can affect one's health and the ability to move easily. In mountainous terrain, weather can change quickly; a fast-moving storm can dump a couple of feet of snow in just a few hours.

Be prepared for all types of weather wet, cold, dry and hot. Take appropriate clothing and the right camping gear. If coming from lower altitudes, spend a few days at higher elevation to allow your body to acclimate.

Be aware of when seasonal heavy snowfall occurs. When trekking into wilderness areas, watch the weather closely and scout escape routes before choosing a campsite. Snow can obliterate trails or make them impassable. It is strongly recommended to never go into a wilderness area alone. Accidents can happen that make self-rescue impossible. Learn how to use a compass, take a map of the area and orient yourself. Let someone know where you are going and when you plan to return.

If you get lost, sit down, regain your composure and think for a few minutes. Many times, people who are lost can figure out where they went wrong and make their way back. If you truly don't know where you are, stay put, establish some form of shelter and initiate your signal plan.

If you are caught in a storm or forced to spend the night out, there are three keys to survival: shelter, fire and signal.

Even if you have nothing else going for you - no fire or food - adequate shelter that is warm and dry will keep you alive until rescuers find you. That means anything from an overhanging rock shelf to a cave, a timber lean-to or snow cave. Always prepare for the worst and build a shelter that will last. Cut boughs from evergreen trees and use them as padding and for covering.

Dress in layers and take extra clothing with you. Put on layers before you become chilled and take off a layer before you become damp with perspiration. Staying warm is a process of staying dry.

AVOID COTTON - cotton becomes wet easily and is difficult to dry. Use wool, wool blends or synthetic clothing that wicks moisture away from skin.

Be sure to carry a cap that is made of wool or synthetic fleece. You lose up to 45 percent of your heat around your head, neck and shoulders. Winter headgear should conserve heat, breathe and be water repellent. The old saying "If your feet are cold put your hat on," is good advice.

Use waterproof foot gear, wool or synthetic socks, and always remember to carry gloves.

Know how to build a fire in wet or snowy conditions. That means carrying a lighter, metal matches or wooden matches in waterproof containers and a firestarter - such as steel wool, cotton or sawdust saturated with paint thinner or alcohol. Camping stores sell a variety of fire starters. Experiment with various materials before going into the field. A fire will warm your body, dry your clothes, cook your food, and help you to signal for help.

Signaling can be done by fire - flames at night or smoke from green branches during the day; with a signal mirror in bright sunshine; and with sound - hence the whistle.

You can live up to three or four weeks without food. You will, however, be more efficient and alert, and have more confidence if you are able to satisfy your hunger, so carry some high-energy food in your survival kit.

Water is more important to survival than food. Your body needs about three quarts of water a day to metabolize its energy reserves and carry away waste. Carry iodine tablets to add to water taken from streams or snow banks. Avoid drinking ice-cold water which will cause your body temperature to drop.

Fatigue and cold causes on to be vulnerable to altitude sickness. Altitude sickness can be mild, severe, or at the worst, it can be fatal. Take time to acclimate and do not move quickly above 8,000 feet. Symptoms of altitude sickness include shortness of breath, fatigue, nausea, headache and loss of appetite. To avoid altitude sickness, get in shape, limit alcohol consumption, acclimate for a few days before the start of the season and drink lots of water. Staying hydrated is a key factor in reducing your chances of getting altitude sickness.

Individuals with any heart problems should be extra careful in high country. If you have a heart condition you should keep any prescribed medication with you at all times. Inform your companions of your condition.

II. Sea Survival: 132 days alone in the South Atlantic [5]

Poon Lim (潘濂; 8 March 1918 – 4 January 1991) was a Chinese sailor who survived 133 days alone in the South Atlantic.

During World War II, Lim was working as second steward on the British armed merchant ship SS Ben Lomond, which was on its way from Cape Town to Paramaribo and New York. The ship was armed but slow moving and was sailing alone instead of in a convoy.

On 23 November 1942, the German U-boat U-172, intercepted and hit the Ben Lomond with two torpedoes. The ship sank in position 00.30°N 38.45°W, approximately 250 miles (400 km) from the nearest land to the south, but ocean currents took him some 750 miles (1,210 km) west to Belém, Brazil, where Lim ultimately landed.

As the ship was sinking, Lim took a life jacket and jumped overboard before the ship's boilers exploded. When the supplies ran low, Lim resorted to fishing, catching seabirds, and rain collection.

---

[5] Tells of 132 Days on a Raft - U.P./New York Times, 25 May 1943
https://www.nytimes.com/1943/05/25/archives/tells-of-132-days-on-raft.html

After approximately two hours in the water, Lim found and climbed aboard an eight-square-foot (0.74 m2) wooden raft. The raft had several tins of biscuits, an 11-gallon (40 liter) jug of water, some chocolate, a bag of sugar lumps, some flares, two smoke pots, and a flashlight. Of the ship's crew of 53, Lim was the sole survivor.

Figure 12-1: Poon Lim, 132 Days on a Raft.

Lim initially kept himself alive by food and water provisions on the raft, but later resorted to collecting rainwater in a canvas life jacket covering and catching fish. He could not swim very well and often tied a rope from the boat to his wrist, in case he fell into the ocean. He took a wire from the flashlight and made it into a fishhook and used hemp rope as a fishing line. He also dug a nail out of the boards on the wooden raft and bent it into a hook for larger fish. When he captured a fish, he would cut it open with a knife he fashioned out of a biscuit tin and dry it on a hemp line over the raft. Once, a large storm hit and spoiled his fish and fouled his water. Lim, barely alive, caught a bird and drank its blood to survive.

At first, he counted days by tying knots in a rope, but later decided that there was no point in counting days and simply began counting full moons.

On 5 April 1943, after 133 days in the life raft, Lim neared land and a river inlet. A few days earlier, he realized that he was nearing land because the color of the water had changed; it was no longer a deep ocean blue. Three Brazilian fishermen rescued him and took him to Belém three days later.

During his ordeal, Lim lost 20 pounds (9.1 kg), but was able to walk unaided upon being rescued. He spent four weeks in a Brazilian hospital while the British Consul arranged for him to return to Britain via Miami and New York.

After his return to the United Kingdom, Lin was awarded a British Empire Medal by King George VI. After the war, Lim emigrated to the United States. When told no one had ever survived longer on a raft at sea, Lim replied, "I hope no one will ever have to break that record." As of 2021, no one has broken Lim's record on a life raft.

III. Air / Jungle Survival: 11 Days in the Peruvian Jungle [6]

Christmas Eve 1971, Juliane Koepcke was flying over the Peruvian rainforest with her mother when their aircraft was hit by lightning. When the aircraft broke in half mid-air, Juliane survived a two-mile fall and found herself alone in the Peruvian jungle.

Figure 12-2: Juliane Koepcke, the Girl who Fell from the Sky.

Snakes, spiders and mosquitos were Juliane's greatest adversaries. She suffered severe sunburn where her dress had ripped. At one point Juliane thought she might lose her arm to an infected wound that infested with maggots.

---

[6] Survival Stories: The Girl who fell from the Sky

http://www.rd.com/true-stories/survival/survival-stories-the-girl-who-fell-from-the-sky/

Juliane Koepcke: How I Survived a Plane Crash - BBC News Magazine, 24 March 2012 http://www.bbc.com/news/magazine-17476615

Juliane walked in streams to avoid poison plants on the jungle floor. Piranhas were a threat, but only in shallow water so she waded mid-stream. Juliane encountered alligators but knew they seldom attacked humans. When on the tenth day she found a boat and a hut, she thought she was hallucinating. Treating her festering wound with gasoline, she pulled out 30 maggots.

The day after finding the hut, Juliane heard the voices of several men outside the hut. Juliane introduced herself in Spanish and explained what had happened. They treated her wounds, gave her something to eat and the next day took her back to civilization.

The day after her rescue, Juliane saw her father. For the next few days, he frantically searched for news of her mother. On 12 January they found her body. She had also survived the crash but was badly injured, couldn't move and died several days later.

IV. Jungle Survival: Plane Crash in the Amazon

Working as a pilot for Brazilian wildcat miners, Antônio Sena (age 36) escaped death when his plane went down in a remote area. He walked through the jungle for 36 days before being rescued.

Sena's ordeal began on Jan. 28, at a small airstrip in Pará state. His task, he said, was to ferry diesel fuel for miners in a remote region where they had built a makeshift landing strip.

Sena was 3,000 feet over the Amazon, flying a small propeller plane on his maiden assignment for wildcat miners deep in the forest, when the lone engine cut out. He took a deep breath and scanned the vast emerald green canopy below. He had about five minutes, he calculated, to bring down the plane and its highly flammable cargo: 160 gallons of diesel fuel.

He reported his imminent crash over a portable radio to whoever might be listening, noting that he was about halfway to his destination, a mine known as California.

Then, as his plane barreled down, Sena aimed for a small valley lined with palm trees.

"There!" he recalls thinking. "Palm trees mean there is water, perhaps a river."

Since becoming a pilot nine years earlier, Sena had heard countless stories about fatal crashes. But while his plane scraped a few trees and then smashed into the ground, Mr. Sena realized something exhilarating as he rolled to a halt: He had survived.

He grabbed a pocketknife, a flashlight, a couple of lighters and a phone with little juice in the battery and scrambled away from the aircraft. Moments later, it burst into flames. Then he settled down to wait for his rescue.

At first, he camped out next to the remains of the 48-year-old Cessna 210L, figuring it was his best chance of being spotted. And search pilots did, in fact, circle the area for several days — and then kept going. He waved and screamed each time he heard the thud of propellers, but to no avail. "They flew right over, but couldn't see me," Mr. Sena said.

Figure 12-3: Antônio Sena (center in black shirt) with Maria Jorge dos Santos Tavares, her two sons and other nut collectors (photo: Antônio Sena).

After he crashed in the Amazon Forest, making fire from mostly damp wood was a daily challenge. Giving up his hopes of being rescued near the wreckage, Mr. Sena embarked on what turned out to be a 17-mile trek through the rainforest, home to jaguars, venomous insects and anacondas – giant serpents that kill their prey (including humans) by crushing to death in their constricting coils.

He turned on his dying phone one final time to launch a geolocation app and then, looking at the map, decided to head in the direction of the Paru River, some 60 miles away. It was the closest area he knew to be inhabited.

For days, Mr. Sena walked only in the morning, using the sun's position to head eastward toward the river. After slogging through swamps and ducking under vines for hours, he would stop in the afternoon to set up a campsite, using palm trees and branches to shelter him from the rain.

Mr. Sena knew that predators usually hunt near the water, where prey is abundant. So he slept on hills. But he was frequently besieged by packs of spider monkeys, which tried to destroy his precarious shelters. "They are very territorial," he said. "I never want to cross their path again."

The monkeys, however, were a godsend: After watching them eat a small, bright pink fruit called breu, Mr. Sena assumed it was safe for human consumption, and it became his main source of sustenance. Besides that, he ate three small, blue eggs from inambu birds, and little else.

One afternoon about four weeks after the crash, when he had gone three days without eating, the buzzing noise of a chain saw stopped him in his tracks. Mr. Sena was excited to hear sound of human activity, but decided it was wisest to stop there for the night. He feared he might get lost if he tried to locate the source of the sound as night fell.

"God, make them use this chain saw again," he prayed before lying down to sleep. The next morning, he heard it again, but only briefly. So he kept walking east, his sights set on the river. On the afternoon of March 6, after 36 days in the Amazon, Sena saw a tarpaulin, and then a man cracking nut besides it. Mr. Sena had stumbled into the campsite of Brazil nut collectors.

By the time Sena emerged from the Amazon jungle, he had lost 55 pounds. Reflecting on his ordeal, Mr. Sena said he walked away with a newfound appreciation for the rainforest. "If I had fallen somewhere in a deserted plantation site, I wouldn't have water, shelter, or what to eat," he said. "The Amazon is so rich."

Afterword

This volume represents knowledge and skills gained from a lifetime of living and working outdoors, beginning as a kid in Southeast Asia and continuing to this day. I can honestly say that I have lived and worked on six continents, and I am alive today because of many of the techniques described herein. Every technique presented in this volume has been validated, often personally under challenging circumstances. It is my hope that the information will serve to prevent misfortune; I can honestly say that the next time a former student approaches me and says, "That thing you taught me saved my life," it will not be the first time.

- pJc

About the Author

Peter Crittenden is a retired US Army Special Forces NCO, with extensive experience in Southeast Asia, Africa, the Middle East, Eastern Europe, Australia, and the Americas. The son of an Australian ex-pat, Pete grew up in Sumatra, Bangladesh and Thailand. During the course of his military career, among other duties Pete served as a survival instructor at the John F. Kennedy Special Warfare Center and School at Fort Bragg, North Carolina. Since retirement from active duty, Pete has worked as a security consultant and personnel recovery advisor for government agencies and corporate clients.

Appendix A

Suggested Inventory: First Aid / Trauma Medical Kit (Note: Acquire proper trauma medical and first aid training; these skills cannot be learned effectively from a book. Suggested training resources include the American Red Cross, Scouting organizations, the military, and first responder / EMT courses at community colleges, etc.)

1. Tourniquet
2. Pressure dressing
3. Z-fold gauze, standard 4.5" x 4 yards
4. Coban roll, standard 2" x 5 yards
5. Trauma shears
6. Band-aids (10x, various sizes)
7. Chest seals (1 pair)
8. Tweezers
9. Irrigation syringe, 20cc with an 18-gauge tip
10. Silk medical tape roll, 1" wide
11. Needle & thread stored in isopropyl alcohol (2x needle/thread, 1x small container)
12. Moleskin, 5" x 2" strip
13. Rolled gauze, standard 4.5" x 4 yards
14. Gauze pads, 4" x 4" (6x)
15. Plastic cling wrap, 2" wide roll
16. Cravat / triangular bandage, 45" x 45" x 63"
17. Butterfly bandages, 0.5" x 2.75" (16x)
18. Safety pins (3x, various sizes)
19. Elastic wrap / ACE bandage, standard 4" x 5 yards
20. Aluminum splint, 36"
21. Emergency blanket (2x)
22. Gloves (2 pairs)
23. Reference guide
24. Abdominal pad (sometimes "ab pad"), 5" x 9" (2x)

25. Nasopharyngeal airway, 28 French (a unit of size used for these devices)
26. White petroleum jelly (Vaseline)
27. Aspirin
28. Acetaminophen (Tylenol)
29. Ibuprofen (Advil)
30. Diphenhydramine (Benadryl)
31. Loperamide (Imodium)
32. Pepto-Bismol pills
33. Caffeine pills
34. Hydrocortisone cream
35. Miconazole (antifungal medication sold under brand name Monistat)
36. Doxycycline and/or Bactrim antibiotics
37. Saline eye drops

Appendix B – NATO Phonetic Alphabet

CHARACTER	MORSE CODE	TELEPHONY	PHONIC (PRONUNCIATION)
A	• —	Alfa	(AL-FAH)
B	— • • •	Bravo	(BRAH-VOH)
C	— • — •	Charlie	(CHAR-LEE) or (SHAR-LEE)
D	— • •	Delta	(DELL-TAH)
E	•	Echo	(ECK-OH)
F	• • — •	Foxtrot	(FOKS-TROT)
G	— — •	Golf	(GOLF)
H	• • • •	Hotel	(HOH-TEL)
I	• •	India	(IN-DEE-AH)
J	• — — —	Juliett	(JEW-LEE-ETT)
K	— • —	Kilo	(KEY-LOH)
L	• — • •	Lima	(LEE-MAH)
M	— —	Mike	(MIKE)
N	— •	November	(NO-VEM-BER)
O	— — —	Oscar	(OSS-CAH)
P	• — — •	Papa	(PAH-PAH)
Q	— — • —	Quebec	(KEH-BECK)
R	• — •	Romeo	(ROW-ME-OH)
S	• • •	Sierra	(SEE-AIR-RAH)
T	—	Tango	(TANG-GO)
U	• • —	Uniform	(YOU-NEE-FORM) or (OO-NEE-FORM)
V	• • • —	Victor	(VIK-TAH)
W	• — —	Whiskey	(WISS-KEY)
X	— • • —	Xray	(ECKS-RAY)
Y	— • — —	Yankee	(YANG-KEY)
Z	— — • •	Zulu	(ZOO-LOO)

Appendix C – Military Phonetic Numerals

1	• — — — —	One	(WUN)
2	• • — — —	Two	(TOO)
3	• • • — —	Three	(TREE)
4	• • • • —	Four	(FOW-ER)
5	• • • • •	Five	(FIFE)
6	— • • • •	Six	(SIX)
7	— — • • •	Seven	(SEV-EN)
8	— — — • •	Eight	(AIT)
9	— — — — •	Nine	(NIN-ER)
0	— — — — —	Zero	(ZEE-RO)

Appendix D – Ground-to-Air Signals

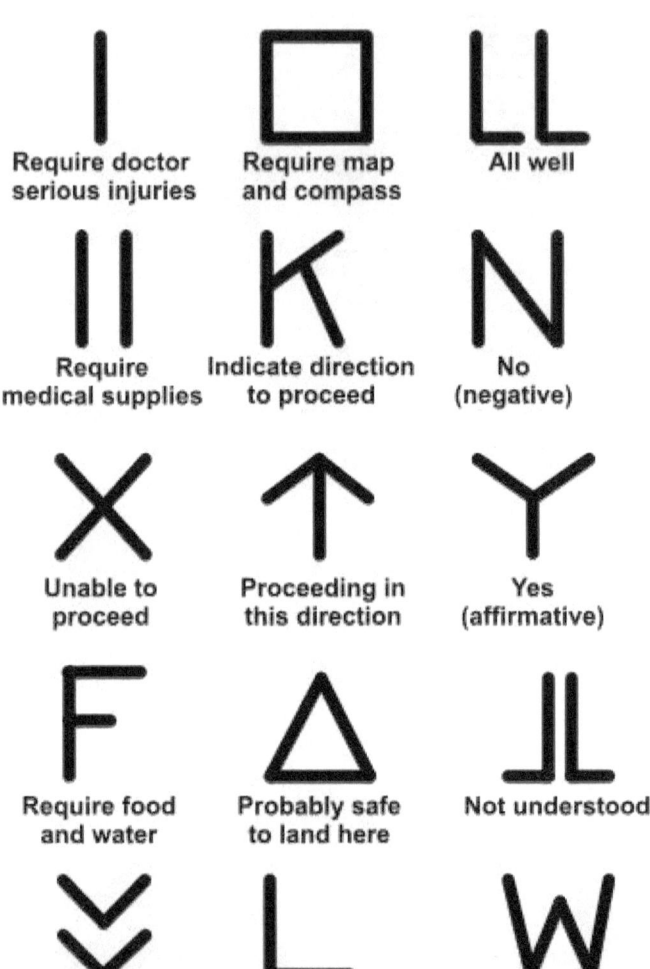

Require doctor serious injuries	Require map and compass	All well
Require medical supplies	Indicate direction to proceed	No (negative)
Unable to proceed	Proceeding in this direction	Yes (affirmative)
Require food and water	Probably safe to land here	Not understood
Require firearms and ammo.	Require fuel and oil	Require mechanic

References

FM 3-05.70 (formerly FM 21-76) SURVIVAL, US Army, May 2002

AFR 64-4, Vol. 1, AIRCREW SURVIVAL TRAINING, US Air Force, July 1985

FM 3-25-26 MAP READING & LAND NAVIGATION, US Army, July 2001

FM 21-18 FOOT MARCHES, US Army, June 1990

FindMeSAR.com https://findmesar.com/

GISsurfer Interactive Maps https://mappingsupport.com/p2/gissurfer-interactive-recreation-disaster-maps.html

How a Personal Locator Beacon (PLB) Can Save Your Life https://tacklevillage.com/how-a-plb-can-save-your-life/

Living Off The Land - A Memorandum on the More Valuable and Common Wild Foods of Europe, Director of Naval Intelligence/Office of Strategic Services, 1943

Reconnaissance Tips of the Trade, Detachment B-52 (Project Delta), Headquarters 5th Special Forces Group, August 1970

SPOT X Two Way Satellite Personal Tracker: https://www.findmespot.com/en-us/products-services/spot-x

The National Map: https://www.usgs.gov/core-science-systems/national-geospatial-program/national-map

The 6 Best Personal Locator Beacons (2021 Reviews): https://www.outsidepursuits.com/best-personal-locator-beacon/

Mayo Clinic - Insect bites and stings: First Aid https://www.mayoclinic.org/first-aid/first-aid-insect-bites/basics/art-20056593

Mayo Clinic - Spider bites: Diagnosis and Treatment https://www.mayoclinic.org/diseases-conditions/spider-bites/diagnosis-treatment/drc-20352377

Mayo Clinic - Scorpion sting: Diagnosis and Treatment https://www.mayoclinic.org/diseases-conditions/scorpion-stings/diagnosis-treatment/drc-20353865

Connect with Blacksmith Publishing

www.thepinelander.com

Other Books by Blacksmith Publishing

Small Unit Tactics Handbook

Fire in the Jungle

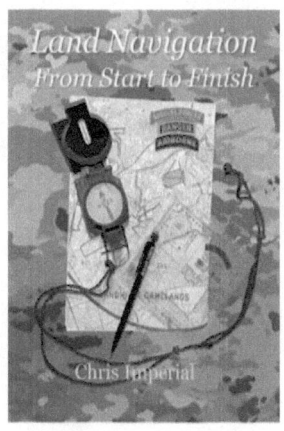

Land Navigation From Start to Finish

Tactical Leadership

www.blacksmithpublishing.com

www.ingramcontent.com/pod-product-compliance
Lightning Source LLC
Chambersburg PA
CBHW021708120626
46545CB00004B/1452